TORTURE TAXI

TORTURE TAXI

*ON THE TRAIL
OF THE CIA'S
RENDITION
FLIGHTS*

*TREVOR PAGLEN
A.C. THOMPSON*

MELVILLE HOUSE PUBLISHING
HOBOKEN, NEW JERSEY

BOOK DESIGN: DAVID KONOPKA

MELVILLE HOUSE PUBLISHING
300 OBSERVER HIGHWAY
THIRD FLOOR
HOBOKEN, NEW JERSEY 07030

WWW.MHPBOOKS.COM

FIRST EDITION, OCTOBER 2006
ISBN: 978-1-933633-09-1

PHOTOGRAPH ON PAGES 40-41 © TONI MARIMON
ALL OTHER PHOTOGRAPHS © TREVOR PAGLEN

A CATALOG RECORD FOR THIS BOOK IS
AVAILABLE FROM LIBRARY OF CONGRESS

TABLE OF CONTENTS

TORTURE TAXI

PROLOGUE

Something happened in the desert. This desert wasn't in Iraq or Afghanistan; it was in Nevada, near the Nevada Test Site, the Southwest's infamous nuclear proving grounds that now doubles as a counterterrorism training area. No one is quite sure why, but, in the early days of December 2002, four planes landed here. The four unusual planes filed flight plans to an obscure landing field at the test site, a place called Desert Rock Airstrip (DRA).

An air traffic controller with a particular interest in "black" military projects was the first to notice the flight plans by using a commercial flight-tracking service and his home computer. The air traffic controller, like others who try to track secret aviation projects, knew that DRA was an important runway to pay attention to. There wasn't usually much activity there. From time to time, Department of Energy-operated aircraft would shuttle to and from the remote airstrip, and these were routine flights. But the air traffic controller monitored DRA for another reason: In addition to being a landing strip for Department of Energy transports, DRA often serves as a "cover story" for flights whose actual destinations are secret. Catch a plane flying to

DRA that isn't operated by the Department of Energy, goes this logic, and there is a good chance that it might be involved in a secret military project.

The Nellis Bombing and Gunnery Range, a huge swath of restricted military land nearly five thousand square miles large, surrounds the Nevada Test Site on three sides and occupies a substantial amount of southern Nevada. Although the Nellis Range is primarily a training facility for Air Force fighter pilots practicing their dog-fighting skills, for bombers finessing their air-to-ground tactics, and for search-and-rescue teams to rehearse their own missions, it is also home to several secret bases. Civilian planes— like contractors and civilian transport services—sometimes have to travel to these bases that "don't exist." And so, as some people have figured out, civilian planes file a flight plan to a legitimate, if slightly obscure, destination like DRA. Once the plane has entered the military airspace above DRA, it resets its radio and transponder frequencies, "disappears" from sight, and quietly proceeds to the "black site" instead of its stated destination. By monitoring aircraft that file flight plans to DRA, one can, from time to time, catch a plane engaging in this kind of subterfuge.

Our air traffic controller had figured all of this out, and he was looking for exactly that—aircraft that might be involved in secret Air Force projects. Suspecting that the four mystery planes, although they had filed plans to DRA, might actually be going to a secret base, he sent out emails to some friends he thought might be interested. He included the planes' tail numbers, the aviation equivalent of a license plate.

The first plane he logged was a civilian version of a Lockheed C-130 cargo plane, popularly known as a Hercules, with the tail number N8183J. A quick search in a Federal Aviation Administration database showed that the plane was owned by an outfit called Rapid Air Trans, Inc., and operated by a Florida-based company called Tepper Aviation. It was arriving from Washington D.C./Dulles Airport.

The second plane was a Cessna 208 with the tail number N403VP. It was owned by a company called One Leasing, Inc., and its operator was unknown.

The third plane was bizarre. It was a Gulfstream IV with the tail number N85VM, and it had arrived from Andrews Air Force Base outside Washington D.C. This plane's owner was a company called Assembly Point Aviation, whose sole proprietor was Phillip H. Morse, a man best known as a co-owner of the Boston Red Sox baseball team. In fact, this Gulfstream usually sported the team's logo on its tail fin. There was no explanation for why the Gulfstream was at Andrews Air Force Base or Desert Rock Airstrip. The plane was soon nicknamed "the Red Sox plane."

The last, and most mysterious, plane was a Boeing Business Jet with the registration number N313P, a brand-new jet that had no distinguishing features except a red-and-blue stripe across an otherwise featureless fuselage. Like the Red Sox plane, the "737 Boeing Business Jet" had arrived from Andrews. A company called Premier Executive Transport Services owned this plane; its operator was also unknown.

In online conversations, a peculiar consensus emerged among the air traffic controllers' fellow aviation researchers: These aircraft probably did land at DRA rather than at one of the secret bases. Something, however, was amiss. Plane number one, the Hercules (N8183J), almost certainly had something to do with the Central Intelligence Agency. The plane's operator, Tepper Aviation, had a history, going back to the 1980s, of working with the agency. The name Tepper Aviation was already attached to a different Hercules that had crashed in Angola while resupplying a CIA-supported rebel faction in 1989.

The second plane, the Cessna N403VP, was another "smoking gun." The plane had become a kind of curiosity the year before when someone photographed it at another secluded airstrip, called Base Camp, in Central Nevada. When aviation enthusiasts had first investigated that sighting, they stumbled upon the fact that its owner, One Leasing, Inc., didn't appear to be a company at all. It took a little while, but they'd realized that One Leasing was also a CIA deception. One Leasing would later show up in conjunction with covert operations in South America.

The third and fourth planes, the Red Sox plane and the 737 Boeing Business Jet, were also peculiar. Evidence was thin, but office gossip at the air traffic controller's job held that these two planes were also connected to the CIA. The two planes, it was said, visited "lots of interesting places."

What this small subgroup of researchers and aviation enthusiasts could not have known at the time was that they had gotten a glimpse into a hidden past and an even more unknown future. On one hand, these planes represented a legacy of secret wars from Africa and South America. On the other, they represented a new secret war, one that was scarcely a year old. This, of course, was the so-called "war on terror," and these four innocuous planes were involved.

These unmarked civilian planes—innocuous-looking business jets and turboprops, painted without any distinguishing features—were operated by a cleverly disguised handful of "civilian" companies. The CIA chose their flight plans, but they were operated by civilian proxies. In a certain way, the commercially available planes were far stealthier than even the most cutting-edge military jets. They didn't need state-of-the-art polymers or precision-designed shapes to hide their identities from enemy radar. Instead, their tactics involved hiding in plain sight. They achieved stealth by looking so boring that no one would bother paying them much attention. And by December of 2002, these unmarked planes had become one of the most important kinds of airpower in the United States' "war on terror." The operations they undertook were some of the Bush administrations' most closely guarded and damning secrets.

These planes, it slowly became known, were connected to a program called "extraordinary rendition," a program to kidnap suspected terrorists and extract information from them at any cost. Suspects were taken to countries where they would be tortured, or brought to a secret network of CIA-operated prisons around the world where the CIA itself practiced torture.

15

Operating under the guise of civilian charter aircraft, these planes could land in places where the United States military would never be welcome. Places like Karachi, Pakistan, Tripoli, Libya, and Banjul, Gambia. But the paper trail that these aircraft left behind would also help trace the outlines of the extraordinary rendition program, hint at secret collaborations in the "war on terror," and provide compelling clues to this secret war's hidden geographies.

After incidents like the one at the Desert Rock Airstrip, aviation hobbyists began paying attention to these planes' movements around the globe. The planes did indeed visit "lots of interesting places." Researchers tracked numerous flights to Guantánamo Bay, to Kabul, and to other known hotspots. Eventually, these and other unmarked airplanes would become collectively known, first to aviation enthusiasts and then to the public at large, as the "torture planes."

As the four planes landed at Desert Rock Airstrip in December of 2002, almost none of this was known to the public. There existed only the faintest rumors of CIA-instigated abductions and torture. "Extraordinary rendition" had yet to become a recognizable phrase. There were only the vaguest indications of CIA kidnappings, of torture-as-policy, of secret "black sites," and of the unmarked airplanes that connected all of these things to one another. But the landings at the Desert Rock Airstrip were a quick glimpse into this new and hidden world, a moment of convergence when a small detail begins to stand in for a massive, yet unseen, presence. The flight logs and the tail numbers from that day were like a small piece of fossilized bone peeking out from the side of a canyon. Something was there, and when researchers began to excavate information about these aircraft, they began uncovering the skeleton of an unknown monster.

I. THE PROGRAM

"The law has been changed," said one of Binyam Mohammed's American interrogators. "There are no lawyers. You can co-operate with us the easy way, or the hard way. If you don't talk to us, you're going to Jordan.... The Arabs will deal with you."[1]

Mohammed had been arrested in Karachi, Pakistan, on April 10, 2002, while trying to leave the country to go to his home in London. He had been in Afghanistan and Pakistan, he insists, to kick a drug habit and to see what a Muslim country looked like. But when Pakistani officials discovered that he was using a passport that belonged to a friend in the U.K., they took Mohammed into custody and handed him over to American interrogators.

For the next few months, Binyam Mohammed was kept in a series of Pakistani prisons, where guards regularly beat him with a leather strap and American interrogators accused him of belonging to Al-Qaeda. This went on for months until two British intelligence agents arrived at the prison. "They gave me a cup of tea with a lot of sugar in it," Mohammed recalled.

"Where you're going you need a lot of sugar," one of the agents told him. Later, said Mohammed, "One of them did tell me that I was going to get tortured by the Arabs."[2]

After three months in Pakistani custody, Pakistani police brought Mohammed to a military airport in Islamabad. Waiting for him was a group of black-clad, masked Americans. The men stripped Mohammed naked, took photos, inserted something into his anus, and dressed him in a track suit, then blindfolded him, placed earphones on him, shackled him, and put him on a plane.[3] He would later be transported to Morocco, Afghanistan, and Guantánamo Bay at the behest of the CIA.

Mohammed had been "rendered," disappeared into a global network of secret prisons, torture chambers, and "black sites" that had been set up with the onset of the "war on terror."

He wasn't the first to be rendered, and he would not be the last.

*   *   *

Six days after September 11, 2001, George W. Bush signed a classified "finding" statement granting the CIA extraordinary powers with which to prosecute a global "war on terror." This still-classified document was part birth certificate, part blueprint for what would become the "war on terror," a guide to a "new kind of war" that would involve new collaborations with foreign governments, new psychological programs, and new paramilitary activities. The document would authorize the creation of a network of secret prisons—"black sites"—around the globe, and it would authorize the CIA to kidnap anyone it suspected of having terrorist affiliations. Age-old complaints about covert actions getting "lawyered" to death would be gone. New, secret wars would begin across the world. Old ones would expand. Strict rules about congressional and executive oversight of covert operations would be a thing of the past. The agency would no longer have to get individual covert actions approved by the President. The CIA would have tremendous new powers and tremendous new autonomy.[4]

To conduct this "war on terror," the agency would quietly collaborate with some of the world's ghastliest regimes. Foreign intelligence services like those of Egypt, Jordan, and Algeria would be pulled into closer contact with the CIA—"bought" through generous subsidies. An "enemy of my enemy is my friend" philosophy would rationalize new relationships with regimes like Libya and Syria. Foreign intelligence services would become CIA proxies and multiply the power and reach of U.S. forces. At the same time, interstate cooperation would help keep American fingerprints off the nastiest incidents, which were bound to occur.[5]

On a Sunday-morning talk show a few days after Bush scrawled his name on the finding statement, Vice President Dick Cheney alluded to what this vision of the future would entail:

> We also have to work sort of the dark side, if you
> will. We're going to spend time in the shadows in
> the intelligence world. A lot of what needs to be

23

done here will have to be done quietly, without any discussions, using sources and methods that are available to our intelligence agencies if we're going to be successful. That's the world these folks operate in.

And so it's going to be vital for us to use any means at our disposal, basically, to achieve our objective....

It is a mean, nasty, dangerous, dirty business out there, and we have to operate in that arena. I'm convinced we can do it....[6]

The disappearances began almost immediately. CIA planes darted around the world virtually undetected, and the CIA had no intention of bringing its prisoners to trial. Instead, men "vanished" into CIA aircraft, and they have rarely been heard from again. On October 23, 2001, a shackled Jamil Qasim Saeed Mohammed disappeared from Pakistan in a white Gulfstream, presumably shipped to Jordan.[7] On November 11, Ibn al-Shaykh al-Libi was flown out of Pakistan to an Egyptian torture chamber.[8] In early December, Abu Faisal and Abdul Aziz disappeared into American hands from Pakistan.[9] On December 18, Ahmed Agiza and Mohammed Zery disappeared from Sweden and were taken to Egypt and tortured.[10] On January 11, 2002, Muhammad Saad Iqbal Madni disappeared into an unmarked Gulfstream in Jakarta, Indonesia, and was taken to Egypt. These were some of the first disappearances in the aftermath of 9/11. There were, no doubt, many more—"After September 11, these sorts of movements have been occurring all the time," an unnamed U.S. official told the *Washington Post*. "It allows us to get information from terrorists in a way we can't do on U.S. soil."[11]

This program of kidnapping is called, of course, "extraordinary rendition." It borrows its name from the common legal process "rendition," which, in law, means "to surrender" or "to return." The name "extraordinary rendition," however, is a euphemism. Although vaguely similar to common rendition processes, *extraordinary* rendition is not defined in international law. In fact, should a person be rendered to a country where torture is likely, the process is decidedly illegal, a clear violation of Article 3 of the United Nations Convention Against Torture.[12] Although the FBI and the CIA have had a program of extraordinary rendition since the mid-1990s, the program's new form is greatly modified and, with the onset on the "war on terror," now routine. Indeed, the covert program has ceased to be "extraordinary" in anything but name. The program is now policy: It's not the exception to the rule but the rule itself.

*   *   *

The CIA aircraft carrying Binyam Mohammed landed in Rabat, Morocco, on July 22, 2002. He was thrown into a van and told to lie down. The van drove for thirty to forty-five minutes.

Mohammed could hear people speaking in Arabic. When the van arrived at its destination, Mohammed was put in a cell in a house that he described as being "dug down, almost underground." There were six rooms: three for prisoners, one for the guards, one for interrogation, and one was empty. He saw that there were already two prisoners in the other cells.[13]

Over the next few weeks, Mohammed was interrogated by Moroccans, but he refused to talk. A white woman named "Sarah," who said she was Canadian also made repeated visits, trying to convince Mohammed to cooperate with his interrogators. Toward the end of July, "Sarah" told Mohammed that "If you don't talk to me, then the Americans are getting ready to carry out the torture. They're going to electrocute you, beat you, and rape you." A few days later, she arrived again at the prison carrying a collection of pictures of top Al-Qaeda leaders. "I don't know these people," Mohammed told her. As "Sarah" left the prison, she told Mohammed, "I'm giving you a last chance to think about cooperating with the U.S."[14]

The night of August 6, three men dressed in all black and wearing black face masks arrived at Mohammed's cell. They chained his hands behind his back and started beating him. "Within ten minutes I was almost gone. It seemed to go on for hours. I had prayed the sunset prayer, but I don't know what time it went on to. I was meant to stand, but I was in so much pain I'd fall to my knees. They'd pull me back up and hit me again. They'd kick me in my thighs as I got up. I vomited within the first few punches. I really didn't speak at all though. I didn't have the energy or will to say anything. I just wanted for it to end."[15]

A week later, Mohammed was transferred to a different prison and held in a white room with a hook on the wall. From his cell, he could hear screams from other prisoners being tortured. Morocan interrogators came to Mohammed's cell regularly to beat him and to tell him what they wanted him to say, what they wanted him to confess to. At one point, the Morroccans arrived, stripped Mohammed naked, and began slicing his chest and penis with a scalpel. The Moroccan men returned once a month to torture Mohammed with the scalpel. Every two weeks, the interrogators returned. They came with pre-prepared lists of confessions for Mohammed, telling him to admit to being a part of Bin Laden's inner circle, to being an Al-Qaeda operations officer, and to advising Bin Laden of targets to attack. Mohammed remained in Moroccan prisons for eighteen months. He was regularly tortured and confessed to various Al-Qaeda activities.[16]

On January 21, 2004, the Moroccans told Mohammed that he was going home. "It was a cold night," he recalled. "I was cuffed, blindfolded, put in a van, and driven for about half an hour. Then they took me into a room, still blindfolded. It was dark." After a few hours, Mohammed heard the sound of an airplane, then of mean speaking American-accented English. "I knew I was being transferred back to the Americans," he said. "It was me and two other prisoners." As they had done in Pakistan, the Americans stripped Mohammed's blindfold and clothes off, and Mohammed saw that he was again surrounded by black-clad Americans wearing face masks. "There was a white female with glasses," he recalled. "She took the pictures. One of the soldiers held my penis, and she took digital pictures. This took a while, maybe half an hour. She was one of the few Americans who ever showed me any sympathy. She was about 5'6", short, blue eyes. When she saw the injuries I had she gasped. She said, 'Oh, my God, look at that!' Then all her mates looked at what she was pointing at and I could see the shock and horror in her eyes."[17] But Mohammed wasn't going home. The Americans were taking him to Afghanistan.

The Boeing Business Jet seen at the Desert Rock Airstrip carried a shackled and blindfolded Binyam Mohammed to Kabul, Afghanistan. "I was put in a truck. I was only in shorts and it was very cold. It seemed like we were driving along a dirt track," he said. After a drive lasting about ten minutes, Mohammed found himself in a CIA prison that has come to be known as the "Dark Prison," or the "Prison of Darkness."

"There was a hall with rooms apart from each other. I am guessing there were about twenty rooms. I was told special people were housed in it, and I was 'special,' which is why I was being taken there. I later found out that these special people were people like Abdulsalam Hiera, the Yemeni businessman from Sana'a, and Dr. Gairat Bahir, the former Ambassador of Afghanistan."[18] Abdulsalam Hiera had been kidnapped by CIA agents from Cairo in September of 2002 and held in Afghanistan as a ghost prisoner.[19]

"They knocked my head against a wall a few times until I could feel blood, then I was thrown into a cell. It was cell number sixteen or seventeen, the second or third last room from the shower room. The room was about two meters by 2.5 meters. The cell had a heavy metal door, all solid, then a second door with bars. There were speakers near the ceilings at both ends of the room. There was a watching hole low down on one wall. There was a hanging pole for people left there in a kneeling position. There was a bucket in the corner for a toilet."[20]

Mohammed described a prison so dark that he couldn't see his hand in front of his face: "It was pitch black, and no lights on in the rooms for most of the time. They used to turn the light on for a few hours, but that only made it worse when they turned it back off."[21]

"They hung me up. I was allowed a few hours of sleep on the second day, then hung up again, this time for two days. My legs had swollen. My wrists and hands had gone numb. I got food only once all this time. After a while I felt pretty much dead. I didn't feel I existed at all." Mohammed was barely alive, but he was taken off the wall and left in the darkness. Like other prisoners who have been kept at the Dark Prison, he described loud music. In Mohammed's words, "Slim Shady and Dr. Dre for twenty days."

"I heard this non-stop over and over, I memorized the music, all of it, then they changed the sounds to horrible ghost laughter and Halloween sounds. It got really spooky in this black hole."[22]

"Plenty lost their minds," recounted Mohammed. "I could hear people knocking their heads against the walls and the doors, screaming their heads off."[23]

*   *   *

Since the rendition program's inception in the mid-'90s, the FBI and the CIA had worked together to capture and prosecute terror suspects. Investigative units at the FBI used the rendition program to bring these suspects to trial in the United States. The FBI almost always took the lead role in these operations, while the CIA played backup, providing intelligence and logistics.

All of this changed on November 11, 2001, when Ibn-Shaykh al-Libi, a "high value detainee" who had allegedly run a terrorist training camp in Khalden, Afghanistan, was captured trying to flee Afghanistan. Immediately, an interagency turf war broke out: The CIA wanted al-Libi in their control. The responsible FBI agent, Jack Cloonan, had early on pleaded with his field agents to "Read the guy his rights," to have his capture "stand as a shining example of what we feel is right." CIA officials felt that Cloonan and the FBI weren't being aggressive enough, and the agency's Kabul station chief passed this complaint to Counterterrorist Center Chief Cofer Black and requested that the CIA take al-Libi from the FBI. Black quickly appealed to CIA Director George Tenet, who, in turn, appealed to the White House, which had already promised the CIA a lead role and significantly expanded powers in the "war on terror."

In January of 2001, the CIA got control of al-Libi. Agents shackled him, placed duct tape over his mouth, and escorted him to an unmarked plane. He was being taken to Egypt. "Before you get there," a CIA agent told al- Libi, "I'm going to find your mother and I'm going to fuck her."[24]

The CIA didn't just get al-Libi, they also won control of the whole rendition program—the FBI was out.[25] And the CIA quickly introduced new tactics, including, most controversially, torture. At first, torture was done by proxy: Al-Libi, for example, was tortured by the Egyptians. Under torture, he told the CIA about connections between Al-Qaeda and Saddam Hussein (information that Colin Powell would later present to the United Nations). Predictably, however, Al-Libi recanted his "confession, which had no basis in fact."[26] But torture was not to be carried out only by proxy nations. As soon as the CIA had established its own "black site" prisons, CIA agents started torturing detainees with their own hands.

In Washington, lawyers at the Justice Department's Office of Legal Council issued statements confirming the legality of these torture practices. Justice Department lawyers Alberto Gonzales, John Yoo, and Jay Bybee had already outlined a legal framework that intended to disintegrate much of the pre-existing law for treating captured detainees. They had created the "unlawful enemy combatant," a person—considered neither soldier nor civilian—with no rights whatsoever and under the complete control of the executive branch. And they had worked to argue that the U.S. naval base at Guantánamo Bay, where many terror suspects were transferred beginning in 2002, was beyond the purview of the U.S. federal court system.

The impetus for the Justice Department's quick work on the torture question came in the form of a query from CIA agents who had tortured a detainee named Abu Zubaydah. Zubaydah was captured in Faisalabad, Pakisan, on March 28, 2002, and rendered to a newly set-up CIA black site in Thailand. Zubayda was suspected of being a top Al-Qaeda officer, but the CIA quickly learned that he wasn't nearly as high an operative as they (and the President) had publicly claimed. Zubayda was little more than an Al-Qaeda logistics operative, charged with making and coordinating travel arrangements and sorting out bureaucratic minutiae. He was a far cry from the terrorist "mastermind" and "architect" that he had been branded. Zubayda also appeared to be mentally ill—his personal diary was written in three different personalities, the work of a schizophrenic.[27] "This guy is insane, certifiable, split personality," FBI agent Dan Coleman later told journalist Ron Suskind.[28]

The CIA agents who had tortured Zubayda sought after-the-fact legal reassurances from the Justice Department that they would not be held liable for torturing prisoners under their control. In a series of memos to Alberto Gonzales, Bybee confirmed this by making several arguments. First, Bybee argued that in order for a technique to qualify as torture, physical pain had to be so great that it was comparable to "organ failure, impairment of bodily function or even death." Psychological torture had to rise to the level of "profound disruption of the senses or personality," which, in Bybee's view, meant that "those acts must penetrate to the core of an individual's ability to perceive the world around him, substantially interfering with his cognitive abilities, or fundamentally alter his personality." Furthermore, Bybee argued, the laws against torture only applied when torture was "specifically intended to inflict severe pain or suffering, whether mental or physical." According to Bybee's argument, a CIA agent charged with torturing someone could claim that their "specific intent" was not to torture their victim but rather to get their victim to talk. He also offered the opinion that an American torturer could claim "self-defense," because if an agent didn't torture the prisoner, following Bybee's logic, he might not learn of an impending attack. Finally, Bybee argued that any attempts to limit the President's interrogation orders would "represent an unconstitutional infringement of the President's authority to conduct war."[29]

When George Tenet told Bush of Zubayda's mental condition and relatively unimportant place in the terrorist organization, Bush replied, "I said he was important. You're not going to let me lose face on this, are you?" After that conversation, Zubayda's American captors began torturing their prisoner, seeking a "breakthrough" that would retroactively validate Bush's claims about Zubayda's importance.[30] The CIA began selectively administering pain medication to its prisoner (Zubayda had been shot in the groin during capture).[31] Even after this torture,

33

however, CIA interrogators were still frustrated by their inability to extract more information from Zubaydah, and they began using more "extreme" methods. They waterboarded Zubayda—a torture technique intended to simulate downing—beat him, threatened him with execution, deprived him of sleep, and blasted him with continuous noise and bright lights.[32] Zubayda began describing scores of terrorist plots—against banks, supermarkets, water systems, nuclear plants, and apartment buildings—none of which could be independently verified.[33]

The CIA, for what it was worth, was in control.

*   *   *

In the course of a police investigation, witnesses are often subpoenaed who have only peripheral knowledge of a criminal act. The logic of this kind of subpoena is that any information about a crime, no matter how inconsequential it may seem, almost always leads to other, and more substantial, information.

The chapters that form the core of this book are, in many ways, modeled on this pattern of investigation. We've focused most of our exploratory efforts on the transport system used to ferry suspected terrorists around the globe—the planes, the companies who own them, and the people who fly them. A book such as this one, written at a time when the Bush administration refuses to confirm or deny even the brute facts of the extraordinary rendition program, cannot give a neatly narrative account of the subject. Perhaps one day, whether through tenacious litigation by journalists, academics, and activists, or through the passage of long decades, the top-secret government documents that one would need to write such a book will become available. At the present moment, such a time seems impossibly far away.

Since 2001, journalists and researchers have examined many parts of the rendition program, and what can most certainly be said today, as the result of nearly five years of investigation, is that the broad outlines of the extraordinary rendition program are no longer a secret. The *Washington Post* filed perhaps the first important report about the program in early March of 2002, and by February of 2005 it was possible for journalist Jane Mayer to publish a long and detailed account of the program in *The New Yorker*. In March of 2005, both the *CBS Evening News* and *60 Minutes* aired stories about CIA renditions. The international press has also been paying close attention. With every new report, more and more information about the program has become publicly available. Those interested in knowing about the CIA's rendition teams can find out quite a lot.

As information has come to light, much has been made about the program as a whole. Some have characterized the rendition program as a massive criminal conspiracy. Early press reports indicated that the CIA had kidnapped well over one hundred detainees.[34] Since some of these detainees were eventually released, the public soon began hearing first-person testimony from those who had been rendered by the CIA. These accounts provided a level of detail and drama that made many start paying attention.

The case described in this chapter was one such testimony: In September of 2005, Binyam Mohammed was transferred to Guantánamo. And there, in November of 2005, he was charged with conspiracy. The government alleged that he had conspired with Al-Qaeda operatives, trained and fought with them in Afghanistan, and, later, met with Jose Padilla and Abu Zubayda in Pakistan to plan a dirty bomb attack on the U.S. which was supposed to, by effect, "free the prisoners" at Guantánamo.[35]

Mohammed has confirmed, through his lawyer, that he did confess to the government's version of the story but adds that his confession was coerced and beaten out of him during eighteen months of torture in Morocco. None of what he confessed to, he now maintains, is true. He says that in actuality he never met Padilla or Zubayda and, because he didn't speak Arabic, couldn't have spoken with them about a Dirty Bomb attack. (The government claims that a translator was present at the meeting in Lahore where they claim Mohammed plotted with Zubayda and Padilla.[36]) Mohammad's lawyer, Clive Stafford Smith, says that there is no evidence against Mohammed that wasn't obtained through torture. Some are skeptical of Mohammed's story, but it resembles, quite closely, the tales of many other detainees who have been rendered.

Perhaps it was the suspicious similarity of the accounts that first caused investigators to pay attention to the program as a whole, but it was the brutality with which individuals had been rendered that caused many to investigate further. The work of the rendition teams seemed to be unusually brutal and, almost always, characterized by excessive force and torture. Although the work didn't seem unusual given the CIA's reputation, it was certainly characterized by a new zeal.

In 2004, lawyers at New York University and the New York Bar Association looked at what was known about the program and argued, unequivocally, that it violated numerous domestic and international laws. In terms of domestic law, they found that "any purported authority to carry out extraordinary rendition would be an unauthorized derogation from U.S. law and policy." On the international front, they found the program violated literally hundreds of laws and regulations, including treaty obligations to which the U.S. was party, such as the UN Convention Against Torture, the International Covenant on Civil and Political Rights, the Geneva Conventions, and the Refugee Conventions of 1951. The lawyers at NYU and the New York Bar Association further found that individuals who authorized, aided, or carried out renditions might be liable to criminal and civil prosecution because they had either "aided or abetted" or "conspired to commit" torture.[37] Nations where the detainees had been kidnapped also began to speak up, complaining that their national laws had been violated, too.

Despite the widespread agreement that the CIA's version of the extraordinary rendition program was illegal, it was clear, almost from the first reports, that it was authorized by the President and

37

justified by elegant, if farcical, legal argumentation. As Anthony Lewis remarked in the *New York Review of Books*, the Bybee torture memos had "read like the advice of a mob lawyer to a mafia don on how to skirt the law and stay out of prison."[38] Because of executive influence, the U.S. courts system consistently refused to consider questions about the program's legality. Where possible, the Bush administration invoked a "state secrets privilege" to prevent U.S. judges from inquiring about the program. And until very recently, the U.S. Congress has refused to even debate such an investigation.

With all of this in mind, we offer the reader a series of journeys in which, like an ongoing police investigation, we try to move closer to the CIA's rendition program by tracking its torture planes.

II. TRACKING TORTURE PLANES

CHAPTER 1 *PAPER AIRPLANES*

Colleen A Bornt

Colleen A Bornt

Signatures. There's something wrong with the signatures on these documents.

A curious quirk of the CIA's fleet of aircraft is that they are civilian, rather than military, planes. Owing to U.S. law and the CIA's status as a civilian agency, the planes are owned by front-companies and operated by a handful of aviation charter companies. One of the consequences of this is that each of these civilian companies leaves a long and voluminous paper trail, much of which is a matter of public record for anyone willing to locate the documents and spend the time sifting through them. We've requested all of these documents and have begun pouring through them. There are registration papers, airworthiness certificates, articles of incorporation, tax stubs, and corporate records, all of which are available from different state agencies (for the companies) or from the Federal Aviation Administration (for the aircraft records). And after pouring through piles and piles of these documents, it's the signatures on them that seem out of place.

Until late 2004, a company called Premier Executive Transport Services owned two of the most active torture planes, but their vice president, a woman named "Colleen Bornt," we now notice, signed her name differently every time she picked up a pen. Her name sometimes appeared in a relaxed and smooth cursive, while at other times, her handwriting was like the jagged strokes of a child. Colleen Bornt's signatures didn't look right because she doesn't exist. In actual fact, the company that she was attached to, Premier Executive Transport Services, is nothing more than a paper company, a front. As others have already discovered, Colleen Bornt, the company's vice president, is a ghost. For us, the fraudulent signatures on these documents confirm the absurdity of it all.

As we look more closely at the corporate documents and aviation filings we've gotten hold of, a landscape begins to emerge. This particular landscape isn't "over there," on the many battlefields of the "war on terror." Rather, the landscape we see depicted in these documents is stealthily and subtly woven into the fabric of everyday life in the United States. While Premier Executive Transport Services' paper trails are filled with distortions, misdirections, and outright lies (they're peppered with forged signatures, people who don't exist, even front companies within front companies), we also see some real places and real names.

One of the only real places we find is 339 Washington Street in Dedham, Massachusetts. This is the address on Premier's letterhead, and it is also the address of a small-time law firm called

Hill and Plakias. Colleen Bornt uses this address, and so does one of the only real people attached to Premier: its lawyer, Dean Plakias.

Left with no one else to ask about Premier, Plakias is the man we are after.

*   *   *

We know that nothing can exist entirely in a vacuum, that even the darkest spaces, the wildest forgeries, and the deepest lies have their material properties, their own internal contradictions. We travel to Boston, rent a car, and drive to Dedham. The trip is premised on the fact that even if 339 Washington is only a front, it can teach us something about the extraordinary rendition program.

Massachusetts is miserable this time of year. It's early March, when the weather is just slightly too warm for snow to fall but spring still seems far away. The streets are filled with thick, wet slush. The skies are a deep gray, and it's raining. Premier's office is on Dedham Square, the closest thing this suburb has to a downtown. Among the red-brick buildings are the Café Fresh bagel shop, Wardle's Pharmacy, and the Armando Cassano Hair Studio. If the weather were nicer, and if there weren't so many SUVs plowing through the winter sludge, we might call Dedham Square quaint. The two-story, red-brick building at 339 Washington St. fits into the nondescript surroundings. On the bottom floor is a Sovereign Bank, whose luminous sign and glowing ATM cast bright reflections on the wet sidewalk.

Around the corner is a Dunkin' Donuts. A worn-out American flag hangs from a nearby house. The law offices of Hill and Plakias, Premier Executive Transport Services' headquarters, are on the second floor. We take the elevator.

Inside, Hill and Plakias' décor is colonial Massachusetts meets the Sharper Image: framed historic documents, pencil-drawn images of founding fathers, and line drawings of clipper ships hang on the walls of the reception area. The firm specializes in family law, but the tone of the office is old-fashioned American justice, Benjamin Franklin more than King Solomon. When the receptionist finishes talking on the phone, she asks how she can help. We're journalists, we explain. "We left messages. Is there anyone here we could talk to about Premier..."

She cuts us off. Her tone has shifted. She becomes hostile. Others, we assume, have been here before, asking the same questions. "There's no one here that you can talk to about Premier Executive Transport Services." There will be no interview with Dean Plakias, the man we had come here to meet.

But that doesn't mean that there isn't more to investigate.

*　　*　　*

In his classic 1974 exposé on the Central Intelligence Agency, *The CIA and the Cult of Intelligence*, former CIA analyst Victor Marchetti recalled Robert Amory, Jr., a high-ranking CIA official, making a point that "if the agency wants to do something in

Angola, it needs the Delaware corporations."[1] The "Delaware corporations" the CIA boss referred to were, of course, the front companies. He'd called them Delaware corporations for the simple fact that most of the CIA's front companies were, and are, organized in Delaware, where lack of corporate regulation is a magnet for businesses of all stripes. (American credit card companies, for instance, are almost always based in Delaware.) But, added Marchetti, "the CIA has not hesitated to use other states when it found them more convenient."[2]

49

The CIA has used front companies, "proprietary organizations," or "proprietaries," as Marchetti called them, for all sorts of activities. When preparing for the Bay of Pigs invasion in 1960, the agency set up a radio station on a remote Caribbean island—Swan Island—to broadcast American propaganda into Castro's Cuba. Radio Swan, as the agency called the station, was operated by a New York company with a Miami address: the Gibraltar Steamship Corporation. When the invasion got underway, Radio Swan switched off the propaganda and started broadcasting orders to the Bay of Pigs invaders and to anti-Castro guerillas on the island. After the failed invasion, the agency transferred ownership of Radio Swan to another front company, the Vanguard Service Corporation, which continued to exist until the late 1960s.[3]

Earlier still than the Bay of Pigs, the CIA used a front company to build the super-secret U-2 spy plane in the mid-1950s. To hide the fact that the Lockheed company was developing the aircraft for the agency, the CIA got the U-2's chief developer, Clarence "Kelly" Johnson, to start a company called "C&J Engineering"—"C&J" being Johnson's initials. The agency then proceeded to pay Lockheed for its work by writing personal checks to Johnson for over a million dollars, money Johnson funneled to his employer. To further hide Lockheed's involvement, Johnson created an address for C&J in California's San Fernando Valley. When enormous shipments of airplane parts started showing up at the nondescript mail drop, a local postmaster got suspicious and began searching public records for the company. When it became clear that C&J wasn't a legitimate business, the postmaster dispatched an inspector to find out where the aircraft parts were actually going. The postal worker showed up at the gates of Lockheed's Skunk Works division, recalled former Skunk Works chief Ben Rich, and "[we] had him signing national security secrecy forms until he pleaded writer's cramp."[4] In 1955, when one of Lockheed's contractors put out a bid for some subcontracting work, one of the subcontractors came back with a warning: "Watch out for this C&J outfit," he said. "We looked them up on Dun and Bradstreet and they don't even have a credit rating."[5] The next year, a pilot named Francis Gary Powers moved to a secret base built by C&J and learned how to fly the U-2 over Nevada before exporting his skills overseas and, ultimately, being shot down over the Soviet Union in 1960.[6]

Today, front companies are far from a thing of the past. Present-day front companies are often only barely more sophisticated than the proprietaries of yesteryear. In 2003, front companies became big news when an outfit called Brewster Jennings and Associates made headlines in connection with CIA operative Valerie Plame. After outing Plame as a CIA operative, right-wing columnist Robert Novak told CNN that Brewster Jennings had been Valerie Plame's "employer" in 1999. His sources for the information were campaign contribution records showing that Plame had donated $1,000 to Al Gore's presidential bid. On the campaign records, Plame had listed her employer as Brewster Jennings. Somewhat more sophisticated than the old C&J of the 1950s, Brewster Jennings came complete with a Dun and Bradstreet rating, but once Novak pulled the thread on Plame's cover, the whole thing started to unravel.[7]

When Robert Amory, Jr., made his comment about "Delaware corporations," he was making an important point about much more than Delaware's lack of corporate regulation. He was pointing out that the CIA couldn't, and cannot, operate entirely in a vacuum or some kind of completely closed-off "black world." The CIA needs a domestic infrastructure to carry out the covert missions abroad. Indeed, front companies are an important part of the CIA's global infrastructure, perhaps just as important to its operations as its forward-deployed stations overseas. The "Delaware corporations" are just as much a part of the agency's capacities as its headquarters in Langley, its training grounds at Camp Peary, or its overseas networks of offices, agents, bases, and airfields. Clandestine infrastructures "over there" can only exist and function by having an analogous infrastructure "over here."

*   *   *

When the CIA wants to set up a front company in order to conduct its business, it has to rely on the same sorts of mechanisms that any legitimate business does. It needs lawyers, addresses, boards of directors, articles of incorporation, shares of stock, and even assets. Someone needs to create the company and state agencies need to authorize its existence. In the case of Premier, the CIA relied on the services of a man named Ralph L. Kissick.

On January 10, 1994, Premier came to exist when Washington D.C. lawyer Ralph L. Kissick, a partner at the Washington D.C. law firm Zuckert, Scoutt & Rasenberger, filed paperwork with the Delaware Secretary of State. Premier, like the front companies that Amory described, was incorporated in Delaware. According to Premier's articles of incorporation on file with the Delaware Secretary of State, the firm's purpose was "to buy, sell, lease, exchange mortgage, acquire, hold, use, improve and/or operate equipment," and "to conduct or engage in any lawful act or activity for which corporations may be organized under the General Corporation Law of Delaware."[8]

Ralph L. Kissick, the man who birthed the corporation by filling those statements back in 1994, has the biography of someone intimately involved in the workings of government.

He graduated from Yale in 1962 and soon after joined the Navy, where he served as an officer until 1966 and, according to his biography, saw "extensive action aboard destroyers in the Atlantic, Mediterranean and Pacific fleets."[9] In 1970, Kissick joined Zuckert, Scoutt & Rasenberger, where he became a partner in 1977. Zuckert, Scoutt & Rasenberger does controversial work, and the firm openly admits on its website that its practice is "concentrated on government contracts, aviation, surface transportation, and related commercial matters." In one lawsuit—a good example of the work the firm takes up—Kissick represented an arms manufacturer named Recon/Optical, Inc., against the government of Israel in a contract dispute.[10] Somewhere along the line, Kissick began doing work for the CIA. We know that he also works with the Department of Defense. As his corporate biography notes, Kissick "helped form and represents a major team of U.S. airlines that provide peacetime airlift services to the Department of Defense."[11]

Like every corporation, Premier also needed a board of directors: officials and managers to run the company. Premier's president was someone named Bryan P. Dyess; its vice president was Colleen A. Bornt; its treasurer was Mary Anne Phister. Another journalist who investigated Premier, Dana Priest of the *Washington Post,* ran these names through an extensive database search and discovered something remarkable: "[The] names turned up none of the information that usually emerges in such a search: no previous addresses, no past or current telephone numbers, no business or corporate records," she reported.

53

Signatures by two members of Premier's ghost board of directors.

"In addition, although most of the names were linked to dates of birth in the 1940s, '50s, or '60s, all were given Social Security numbers between 1998 and 2003."[12] In other words, aside from Kissick, who filed Premier's articles of incorporation, and Massachusetts lawyer Plakias, Premier's "registered agent," none of the people associated with the company actually exist in the flesh—Premier is only a collection of ghosts.

Kissick has also created other front companies on behalf of the CIA, many of which have been implicated in the extraordinary rendition program. One company was Crowell Aviation (which also resides in Plakias' law office). Another was Stevens Express Leasing. The ghost board of directors from Premier showed up on some of these companies' boards as well. A ghost named Phillip P. Quincannon, for example, was an officer of Premier, Crowell, and Steven's Express Leasing. A sterile identity named Erin Marie Cobb—an officer at Stevens Express Leasing—extended the web of fake companies to two other front companies, Devon Holding and Leasing, and Rapid Air Transport. These two companies were creations of another CIA proxy: a Maryland lawyer named Douglas R. Thomas.[13] The names of all of these companies are all intimately enmeshed with the rendition program's labyrinthine paper trail.

And the companies, should we choose to call them that, sometimes run right into each other: When Premier's 737 Boeing Business Jet abducted a German citizen in Macedonia, for example, the aircraft identified itself to European air traffic controllers as being operated by not Premier but "Stevens Express Leasing."[14]

55

8-1

Aviation Specialties, Inc.

Box 9831   Friendship Station   Washington, DC 20016
Telephone: (202) 783-1619

0 0 0 0 0 0 0 0 2 7 2

PREMIER EXECUTIVE TRANSPORT SERVICES, INC.
339 WASHINGTON STREET
SUITE 202
DEDHAM, MASSACHUSETTS 02026
TELEPHONE: (617) 326-8848

P

8068V 64
379P

10 SEP 15 2003

0 0 0 0 0 0 0 1 5 2 1

CROWELL AVIATION TECHNOLOGIES, INC.
339 WASHINGTON STREET
SUITE 202

P.O. BOX 632
DEDHAM, MASSACHUSETTS 02027-0632

TELEPHONE : (617) 326-8848

$$\frac{-64}{\frac{1016m}{319\Omega}}$$

July 12, 2002

10 AUG 0 2 2002

---

0 0 0 0 0 7 0 1 4 7 7

217

Devon Holding & Leasing, Inc.
23 West Second Street, Lexington, North Carolina 27292
Tel: (910) 243-2730

$$\frac{-64}{\frac{3190}{7248}}$$

10 FEB 23 1999

February 4, 1998

*   *   *

Documents on file with the states of Delaware and Maryland show that Premier was transferred to Dean Plakias' Dedham address in 1996. The company then lay dormant until 1999. CIA aviation firms like Premier, however, don't remain paper companies for long. They need to acquire airplanes, so, in 1999, the ghost Colleen Bornt began signing documents to take delivery of a brand-new Gulfstream V jet on Premier's behalf. As Bornt penned her spectral name to aircraft registration documents, Premier emerged from its dormancy and came to life. Its tail number was N379P; its serial number 581.[15] This purchase came almost two years before the "war on terror" began. When this Gulfstream started flying after 9/11, it earned the nickname "the Guantánamo Bay Express" because of its frequent trips to the American prison.

Within a few weeks of being granted newfound powers (and funding) with the onset of the "war on terror," the CIA procured another aircraft through Premier. This was the 737, the Boeing Business Jet. On December 20, 2001, another one of Premier's ghosts—"Bryan P. Dyess"—finalized the purchase of this brand-new plane directly from Boeing.[16]

According to FAA records, the Business Jet spent the better part of 2002 undergoing various kinds of maintenance and modifications to the factory-delivered plane. The DeCrane Aircraft Systems Integration Group, of Georgetown, Delaware, which describes itself as "[providing] the highest level of personal service for VIP and Head-of-State aircraft," outfitted the plane with a pair of "winglets"—performance-enhancing vertical fins on the plane's wingtips—and installed a proprietary auxiliary fuel tank system. Later that year, the Associated Air Center in Dallas, Texas, installed an "executive interior" and a Canadian Marconi SATCOM antenna system in the plane.[17] Aviation enthusiasts would eventually take note of the various "bumps" and "antennas"—the telltale signs of enhanced communications systems—on the aircraft's fuselage.

*   *   *

No one was supposed to have noticed the secret work being done by Premier's planes, but almost as soon as they began darting around the world after September 11, they were involved in a number of incidents that made them stand out as suspicious.

The first occurred on October 23, 2001, in Karachi, Pakistan. Sometime around 2:40 a.m., a rented Toyota sedan arrived at a quiet corner of the airport. A group of masked agents from Pakistan's Inter-Services Intelligence Agency, the ISI, led a shackled man named Jamil Qasim Saeed Mohammed out of a Toyota and handed him over to a group of Americans waiting near a bone-white Gulfstream V. The prisoner was a Yemeni microbiology student suspected of being involved in the October 2000 bombing of the USS *Cole*. None of the usual deportation or extradition proceedings had taken place—the Americans simply grabbed the man, threw him into the waiting aircraft, and planned to disappear into the night sky in an operation meant to be over in minutes.[18] (At the time, no one knew where the plane was heading, although subsequent reports put the plane's destination as Jordan.[19])

But there was a problem: The plane's operators had refused to pay the airport's requisite landing fees. In turn, the air traffic controllers denied the Gulfstream permission to depart. The plane sat on the tarmac as a standoff ensued. Pakistani intelligence officers finally intervened, forcing airport officials to capitulate, and the Gulfstream was allowed to take off.[20] But the incident had attracted attention. Three days later, Pakistani journalist Masood Anwar learned of the incident and published the tail number of the plane that had been observed waiting on the tarmac that night. It was Premier's N379P, the Guantánamo Bay Express.[21] It was a simple, innocuous fact, this tail number, but with this simple fact, Anwar began pulling on a thread that, in the hands of other journalists, would begin to unravel more and more clues to the extraordinary rendition program.

On December 18, 2001, eight weeks after the late-night abduction from Karachi, Premier's Guantánamo Bay Express showed up again—this time in Bromma, Sweden. Earlier in the day, the Swedish Security Police, the Sakerhetpolisen (SÄPO), had intercepted and arrested a man named Ahmed Agiza on his way home from a Swedish-language class in Karlstad. They also arrested a man named Mohammed Zery, who was, at the time of his arrest, shopping in Stockholm. A few hours later, a SÄPO agent placed a call to the police station at the Bromma airport, asking for assistance with two suspected terrorists who were going to be arriving shortly at the airport. Before long, a group of SÄPO arrived at the airport and were waved in. Next, two Americans wearing civilian clothes showed up at the airport police station and stood around chatting with the Swedish authorities. Swedish policeman Paul Forell remembers believing that they were from the American embassy. That evening, Premier's Gulfstream V landed on the tarmac. A Swedish officer walked up to greet the crew of about six masked Americans and two Egyptians. "I told them that you don't need to wear hoods because there is no one here," recalled the officer, but the hoods stayed on. Soon thereafter, a SÄPO car arrived at Gate K. Then Agiza and Zery, in chains, were led into the airport police station. The masked Americans were waiting for them.[22]

Earlier that day, Swedish government ministers had scheduled an impromptu meeting in which they voted to expel Agiza and Zery based on secret evidence provided in part by foreign intelligence services, although the Swedish government refused to disclose the evidence or to say where it had come from. SÄPO wanted to expel the men as quickly as possible—so that they wouldn't have a chance to appeal their extradition—and had tried to book a charter flight to Egypt from a company called Executive Air. However, the plane wouldn't be able to fly until the following morning. SÄPO agents felt that that was too long and so they turned to the CIA for help. The CIA told the Swedes that they had a private jet waiting in Cairo for exactly these sorts of operations—it could fly on a moment's notice. At 2:30 that afternoon, Premier's Gulfstream, the Guantánamo Bay Express, took off from Cairo.[23]

Even before the plane had landed in Sweden, tensions had started to develop between the CIA and the Swedish authorities. While waiting at the airport, the American Embassy officials had told the Swedes that there wasn't enough room on the plane for them to accompany the prisoners to Cairo. The Swedes protested and were ultimately given two seats. A Swedish security officer "felt that [the CIA] were backing into our territory."[24]

When Agiza and Zery arrived at the airport, the Americans insisted on strip-searching the prisoners. Again, the Swedes protested—they had already searched and chained the prisoners. The plane's captain told them that the aircraft wouldn't take off unless the Swedes allowed its crew to conduct the operation their way. Working silently and communicating with hand signals, the Americans sliced the prisoners' clothes off and searched them again while another agent took photographs. The Americans inserted suppositories into Agiza and Zery's anuses, put diapers on them, zipped them into gray jumpsuits, and covered their heads with hoods. Agents then chained Agiza and Zery to a harness in the plane. At 9:49 p.m., the plane was headed back to Cairo. "Everything was very smooth," recalled Swedish officer Paul Forell. "I thought, 'They have done this before.'"[25]

When Agiza and Zery arrived in Egypt at 3 a.m., a series of brutal interrogations at the hand of Egyptian security began immediately. According to family members, attorneys, and Swedish diplomats, the two men reported that they were tortured repeatedly over the next several months—including the administration of electrical shocks by electrodes attached to their bodies, a form of torture designed to prevent leaving marks on a victim's body.[26]

After almost two years in prison, the Egyptians released Zery in October 2003. They had determined that he had no substantial ties to terrorism, but confined him to his native village in Egypt and kept him under constant surveillance nonetheless. In April 2004, the Egyptian government sentenced Agiza to a twenty-five-year prison term for his membership in the Egyptian Islamic Jihad, an organization outlawed in Egypt. The trial was conducted behind closed doors. Agiza maintains that he cut his ties to Islamic Jihad in the early 1990s, and no evidence contradicting this claim has been presented to the public.[27]

In May of 2004, Swedish journalists working on a documentary about Agiza and Zery's abduction from Sweden discovered Massachusetts lawyer Dean Plakias' connection to the mysterious aircraft used in the operation. Journalist Fredrik Laurin was able to get Plakias on the phone. The lawyer referred Laurin to a certain "Mary Ellen McGuiness," whose 703 area code indicated she was in northern Virginia. Laurin posed as a potential customer interested in chartering an airplane, but McGuiness told the journalist that "we only lease to the U.S. government" and that the plane was on a "long-term lease with them."[28] "Let me see if I can find someone to call you back," said McGuiness. Fifteen minutes later, Laurin's phone rang. It was Mikael Londström from SÄPO, inquiring about Laurin's call to unnamed "U.S. authorities."[29]

*   *   *

The seeds of the rendition program were first planted in the 1980s, and operations began in the 1990s. That is, the program had gestated under the Reagan administration and come to life under Clinton. With the beginning of the "war on terror," its scope exploded overnight, but the program was already squarely and solidly in place.

It is commonly forgotten that the "war on terror" did not begin with the Bush administration but began, instead, under Ronald Reagan.[30] International terrorism first became a prominent issue in American foreign policy after a succession of terrorist attacks on Americans overseas: In 1983, a suicide bomber attacked the American Embassy in Beirut, killing sixty-three and wounding more than a hundred others. Later that year, 241 Marines were killed by a car bomb, also in Beirut. In 1984, terrorists kidnapped, tortured, and killed the CIA's Beruit Chief William Buckley. In 1985, terrorists hijacked the cruise ship *Achille Lauro* off the coast of Egypt, killing an American passenger; earlier that year, a U.S. Navy diver was executed when members of Hezbollah hijacked TWA flight 847 from Athens to Rome; and bombings at airports in Rome and Vienna killed several more Americans.

Amid this wave of terrorist attacks against Americans, Congress gave the Federal Bureau of Investigation power, in 1986, to investigate attacks against Americans that occurred outside the United States. Three years later, the FBI was given power to extradite people from foreign countries without the host countries' consent.[31] But even before that, in 1981, President Reagan signed Executive Order 12333, which granted the CIA the power to "provide specialized equipment, technical knowledge or assistance, or expert personnel for use by any department or agency." It also allowed the agency, although prevented by law from making arrests, to "render any other assistance and cooperation to law enforcement authorities not precluded by applicable law."[32] Concurrently, a task force headed by Vice President—and former CIA head—George H.W. Bush recommended creating a Counterterrorist Center (CTC) within the CIA where representatives from various government agencies could consolidate and collaborate on anti-terrorism efforts. The Center would bridge the CIA's Directorate of Operations (the covert-action arm of the agency) with the Directorate of Intelligence (the agency's analysis arm). Although the CTC would issue analyses and reports, its focus was squarely on operations.[33]

Before the second Bush administration's "war on terror," the highest-profile rendition occurred on February 8, 1995, when

65

agents from the FBI's Joint Terrorism Task Force took custody from Pakistani authorities of Ramzi Yousef, whom the State Department described as the "most wanted man in the world" for his role in the 1993 World Trade Center bombings. The previous day, Pakistani commandos had captured Yousef at the Su Casa guesthouse in Islamabad. He'd been on the run for several years, hiding in the Philippines and Pakistan. Agents from the CIA's Counterterrorist Center charged with tracking Yousef had uncovered a major lead the previous month. When a fire broke out at the Tiffany Mansion apartments in Manila, Philippine police found one of Yousef's childhood friends, Abdul Hakim Murad, in an apartment Yousef had just fled. They also found evidence of bomb-making materials and Yousef's laptop with a collection of encrypted computer files. The computer files on Yousef's laptop contained evidence of a plot to bomb American commercial jets over the Pacific Ocean. The Philippine police proceeded to torture Murad for the next sixty-seven days, generating numerous "confessions" that a Filipino officer would later describe as police fabrications that Murad had agreed to in order to end the pain.

A year later, Yousef, Murad, and a third man, Wali Khan Amin Shah, were tried and convicted of conspiracy charges in a New York Federal court. But Yousef was part of a larger network of people whose names in 1996 were still unfamiliar to most Americans—his guest house in Pakistan was funded by Osama Bin Laden, and the Manila apartment belonged to Khalid Sheikh Mohammed, the "architect" of 9/11.[34]

Nineteen ninety-five saw the Clinton White House reaffirm and expand the nascent rendition program. Terrorism had once again appeared in the domestic consciousness: After Ramzi Yousef was apprehended, he made grandiose claims about all of the plots he had been planning. His threats filled the newspapers, and when, in April 1995, the Oklahoma City Federal Building was bombed, many commentators initially and incorrectly blamed the bombing on Islamic terrorists. Later came the Japanese Aum Supreme Truth cult gas attack on the Tokyo subway system. These incidents prompted the Clinton administration's first terrorism policy review, which led to Presidential Decision Directive 39: "When terrorists wanted for violation of U.S. law are at large overseas, their return for prosecution shall be a matter of the highest priority... return of suspects by force may be effected without the cooperation of the host government." In other words, the rendition program was reaffirmed, and the United States was recommitted to it.

But the rendition program was still essentially guided by the "law-enforcement" approach to international terrorism, and to prepare for a rendition meant getting an indictment against a suspect, seeking cooperation from the host country where the suspect was thought to be hiding, and engaging in surreptitious kidnapping only when host countries proved uncooperative.[35] But just as the FBI was taking the lead in these "renditions to justice," as renditions to the United States have become colloquially known, the CIA itself had begun another rendition program—"extraordinary rendition."

67

There were strong feelings at the CIA, however, that its operating procedures were fundamentally incompatible with the dictates of a U.S. trial. The head of the CIA's new Bin Laden desk, Michael Scheuer, described the frustration: "We knew where these people were, but we couldn't capture them because we had nowhere to take them."[36] The Clinton administration's answer to this impasse was to authorize the CIA to take prisoners to third countries, usually Egypt. In practice, this meant "disappearances" and, inevitably, torture. Egypt provided an obvious solution to the CIA's dilemma. Except for a brief period in the early 1980s, the country has been ruled under "emergency laws" since 1967—laws that consolidate power in the president and which authorize Egyptian authorities to detain suspects for long periods of time without trial, refer civilians to unconventional "State Security Emergency Courts," censor media in the name of national security, and prohibit unauthorized political activities. Egyptian prisons are notorious for torture. But Egypt is also the second largest recipient of U.S. foreign aid, and the CIA has maintained close collaboration with the notorious Egyptian secret police, the Mukhabarat. The Egyptian leader, Hosni Mubarak, had been fighting Islamic extremists in his own country ever since he'd taken power after the 1981 assassination of Anwar Sadat by members of the Islamic Jihad. It was convenient that many of the suspected members of Osama Bin Laden's growing Al-Qaeda organization happened to be Egyptian. The CIA made it clear to the Mukhabarat that it had all the resources it needed (including a fleet of airplanes) to find and capture terrorism suspects—it just needed a place to bring them. Egypt agreed to the plan. On September 13, 1995, the CIA kidnapped terror suspect Talaat Fouad Qassem from Croatia and delivered him to Cairo. Qassem hasn't been heard from since; he's believed to have been executed.[37]

Over the next several years, Scheuer and his colleagues at the CIA's Counterterrorist Center formalized the rendition program. In 1997, they established a Renditions Branch within the center.[38] They set up teams specifically designed to conduct rendition operations. Rendition became an institutional capacity—something that the CTC was capable of doing. The CTC wasn't under any illusions about the fact that its prisoners would likely be tortured in Egypt or other countries to which they'd be delivered. "Each time a decision to do a rendition was made," recalled Scheuer, "we reminded the lawyers and policy makers that Egypt was Egypt, and that Jimmy Stewart never starred in a movie called *Mr. Smith Goes to Cairo*."[39] Administration lawyers and policy makers, said Scheuer, "inserted a legal nicety by insisting that each country to which the agency delivered a detainee would have to pledge it would treat him according to the rules of its own legal system."[40] In February 2000, George Tenet testified that the U.S. had participated in the rendition of two dozen terrorists since July 1998—some were brought to the U.S. to stand trial, he said, but most were delivered to other countries.[41] Two years later, Tenet testified to the 9/11

69

Commission that the CIA had participated in seventy renditions before September 11, 2001.[42] In 2002, a year after the administration of George W. Bush had given the CIA "exceptional" authorities, the CIA's Counterterrorist Chief Cofer Black famously testified regarding the "operational flexibility" of the Counterterrorist Center: "This is a highly classified area. All I want to say is that there was 'before' 9/11 and 'after' 9/11. After 9/11 the gloves came off."[43]

*   *   *

When, in early 2005, *60 Minutes* visited the law offices of Hill and Plakias, they called Premier a "dead end." In some ways, it was, but the information we have been able to gather about the firm is instructive, for it provides an important case study in the structures at work in the CIA's extraordinary rendition program. Although Premier wasn't a product of September 11, or a newly set up front, it was certainly a working piece of the rendition program and important to the way the program functioned.

Researchers and journalists have been able to investigate Premier's planes because of a peculiar contradiction in the way that the CIA is set up. Because the CIA's work, including the rendition program, is conducted by civilian means—the agency might employ the assistance of the military, but it is not itself a branch of the military—the CIA has traditionally conducted many of its activities by hiding in plain sight. Its agents pretend

UNCLASSIFIED

Within the United States, we shall vigorously apply U.S. laws and seek new legislation to prevent terrorist groups from operating in the United States or using it as a base for recruitment, training, fund raising or other related activities. (U)

o Return of Indicted Terrorists to the U.S. for Prosecution: We shall vigorously apply extraterritorial statutes to counter acts of terrorism and apprehend terrorists outside of the United States. When terrorists wanted for violation of U.S. law are at large overseas, their return for prosecution shall be a matter of the highest priority and shall be a continuing central issue in bilateral relations with any state that harbors or assists them. Where we do not have adequate arrangements, the Departments of State and Justice shall work to resolve the problem, where possible and appropriate, through negotiation and conclusion of new extradition treaties. (U)

If we do not receive adequate cooperation from a state that harbors a terrorist whose extradition we are seeking, we shall take appropriate measures to induce cooperation. Return of suspects by force may be effected without the cooperation of the host government, consistent with the procedures outlined in NSD-77, which shall remain in effect. (S)

o State Support and Sponsorship: Foreign governments assist terrorists in a variety of ways. (U)

UNCLASSIFIED

to be embassy employees, its procurement contracts look as if they come from legitimate companies, and its aircraft act like charter planes.

As far as its airplanes are concerned, the CIA agents gain distinct advantages over their military counterparts. Business jets like those belonging to Premier have a different kind of camouflage than their military counterparts. They look utterly unimportant, hopelessly ordinary. When a U.S. military transport lands in some unlikely part of the world, people notice and inevitably inquire what the U.S. military is doing in a particular location. Business jets don't have the same sorts of problem—they don't call attention to themselves, and spotting an unusual civilian plane requires an intimate familiarity with civilian aviation norms.

The use of civilian planes also allows the CIA to take advantage of national and international aviation conventions. Civilian aircraft are granted far more operational flexibility than their military counterparts, owing to a series of international agreements that are collectively known as the Convention on International Civil Aviation, more commonly known as the Chicago Convention. The Chicago Convention grants civilian aircraft the right to fly over airspace controlled by signatory nations. In general, civilian aircraft do not need specific permission to enter the airspace of another country—a private pilot from Montana can, for example, fly over Canadian airspace at will, provided that she obeys the necessary flight rules. The Chicago Convention doesn't apply to military flights, which always need specific clearances to enter foreign airspace.[44] Again, being a civilian provides a degree of "cover" and a degree of flexibility.

One of the ironic things about front companies is that they have to make a minimal effort to look like regular companies, and this means leaving the long paper trail that we've been able to follow. These corporate records are not secret. Add an airplane to a particular company's operations, and its paper trail grows exponentially. Because the airline industry is highly regulated, the FAA keeps records on the registration histories for all U.S.-based aircraft, as well as a history of all modifications to civilian-owned aircraft. All of these records, designed to make the skies safer by helping to ensure the airworthiness of the planes in the skies (and the identities of those flying them) are accessible to the public. If anyone wants to know the history of an aircraft they're considering purchasing, or are unsure about the airworthiness of a particular plane, open records are there to provide the information.

One of the first journalists in the United States to follow the Guantánamo Bay Express' tail number back to the Dedham law offices of Dean Plakias was Farah Stockman of the *Boston Globe*. She was able to interview Dean Plakias before he stopped talking to the media. When she found Plakias, she found a relatively low-profile suburban attorney. "He's basically a divorce lawyer," Stockman told us from her office phone in Washington D.C. "I have no idea why the CIA chose to hide behind Dean Plakias, or how much they paid him," she said. While preparing her story for the *Globe*, one of the things that Stockman wanted to

73

emphasize was that the infrastructure behind the torture planes was almost exceptionally banal: Plakias was a normal guy, the kind of guy "who takes his kids to soccer practice." But Plakias insisted on keeping his own life out of Stockman's story and declined to answer most questions about his involvement with the front company.[45]

And, although Stockman found Plakias to be pleasant enough, she learned little about Premier. "I asked about why the company had moved to Massachusetts from Delaware, but he wouldn't give a lot of details," she told us. Stockman is still unsure about how or why Premier ended up in this particular corner of suburban Massachusetts, or the extent of Plakias' involvement with the company. "Did Dean Plakias really have anything to do with rendition?" asked Stockman. "I have no indication that he knew what was happening, but he certainly knew that he was operating on behalf of the CIA."[46]

CHAPTER 2 *A TOWN CALLED SMITHFIELD*

The small town of Smithfield is a half-hour drive from Raleigh, North Carolina. It is nestled between countless acres of spindly pine trees and the languid, muddy currents of the Neuse River. In town, the company Aero Contractors operates in the open. Aero does work for the CIA, and many of its employees live in town. Smithfield, you might say, is a company town, and we are interested to see it up close.

As we drive toward the town of about twelve thousand, which is located in rural Johnston County, signs illustrating a regional ethos began piling up, one upon another. A bar called The Last Resort, which is on the outskirts of town, is draped in Confederate flags. We see war memorials everywhere. The county courthouse, which is closed for Good Friday, is adorned with five of these memorials and, additionally, plaques commemorating two different Civil War battles. Across the street, the Riverside Coffee Company displays a framed letter of appreciation from the members of an Army company stationed at nearby Fort Bragg. As we drive farther into town, we see billboards and neon signs that proclaim, over and over again, that Jesus is Lord, that He saves, and that everlasting damnation is always only a few misplaced steps away. There are churches everywhere.

But things are sometimes amiss in God's Country: Novels and horror movies are filled with clichés about small towns. In these tales, small towns quite often hold a deep and terrifying secret. And although what goes on at the Johnston County Airport isn't quite *Children of the Corn*, it isn't far behind. Smithfield, like many small towns, is home to a few things better left unsaid.

We are interested in what goes on at the local airport. The Johnston County Airport is a small regional facility on the outskirts of Smithfield. It's little more than a runway next to a small collection of hangars, trailers, and sheds. Most of the planes housed here are Cessna prop planes piloted by local aviation enthusiasts. But Aero Contractors, Ltd., also operates out of the airport. It runs its operations from a small area south of the runway at the end of a side street called Charlie Day Memorial Drive. (The street name hints at Aero Contractors' business: Charlie Day was a mechanic for the CIA front Air America.) While front companies like Premier Executive Transport Services actually own the CIA's fleet of torture planes, Aero Contractors is one of the companies that controls and flies them.

And so it is that this small, rural airport in the heart of Johnston County is the last stop of countless CIA rendition flights. One of the most infamous torture planes, the Gulfstream V known as the Guantánamo Bay Express, called this place home for five years. A small fleet of Spanish-made Casa turboprops, which have been spotted all over the world, is stationed here as well. A Twin Otter, with the tail number N6161Q, that Aero operates makes regular flights to the CIA's training grounds at Camp Peary. Aero Contractors also operates the infamous 737 Boeing Business Jet from a nearby airport in Kinston, North Carolina.

*   *   *

Walt and Allyson Caison are some of the very few people living in Johnston County willing to talk to us about the CIA's operations at the local airport. They are vocal about the topic, and they are very critical. As deeply committed Christians, the Caisons were profoundly disturbed when in May 2005 the news show *60 Minutes* did an exposé on the case of Khaled El-Masri. El-Masri is a German citizen who was kidnapped while vacationing in Macedonia; he was eventually taken to a secret CIA prison in Afghanistan and tortured. *60 Minutes* had implicated Aero Contractors and Johnston County Airport in his disappearance and subsequent torture. While the Aero pilots and personnel living in the Caisons' community probably did not kidnap suspected terrorists off the streets—nor would they likely have been trusted to apply torture—they had, we know, flown the getaway planes. And Walt and Allyson know that the parents of their children's friends had delivered hooded, drugged, and shackled prisoners to some of the war on terror's darkest spaces. What's more, these flights always came back to Smithfield;

the torture planes' home base was the Caisons' backyard.

Walt, a middle-aged psychologist with a bushy mustache and gentle eyes, had known about the airport for a long time. He first heard about Aero Contractors while on a Boy Scout camping trip with his son. Late one night, around the campfire, one of the other dads brought up the "the CIA-run operation out at the airport." Walt didn't push the issue, wary of offending the other men's deep conservatism. The CIA's presence in Smithfield was an open secret, said Walt: "Everybody in town has known for years that there was a company out there that flies operations for the CIA."[1]

"I come at this from a faith-based perspective—what's right is right," Allyson told us.[2] The Caisons understood their faith to contain a message of justice, an obligation to stand against injustice and treat others with decency no matter what they had done. It was hard to imagine anything more non-Christian than disappearing and torturing people, they reasoned. But Aero's presence in the county, not to mention the work the company was involved with, was not a topic for public discussion, they told us. What little talk there was among the Caison's neighbors and church congregation revolved around whether the Bible permitted torture. A number of people at the Caisons' church were quite certain it did. They pointed out that God ordered swarms of locusts to torture nonbelievers in the book of Revelation.

For Walt and Allyson Caison, speaking about disappearances and torture in Johnston County is less abstract than it is on the pages of the *Washington Post* or the *New York Times*. To speak against torture in Smithfield is to speak, quite literally, against the actions of one's neighbors. Everyone in Smithfield knows each other, their neighbors, and their neighbors' neighbors. And Aero is a major employer in the region. For the Caisons, speaking to us about torture was akin to accusing their townspeople of participating in a satanic conspiracy. Moreover, the odds were heavily stacked against dissent. Aero's board, they told us, is composed of the town's business and church leaders, lawyers, and other prominent members of the small community. The deacon of the Caisons' church sat on Aero's board, as did many of Smithfield's "well-respected community members," said Allyson.

*   *   *

Aero Contractors' assistant manager, who actually runs the company, is a man named Bob Blowers. And like so many of those involved in the extraordinary rendition program, he has maintained that Aero Contractors has absolutely nothing to do with the CIA, much less torture and disappearances. When the local press began asking questions about Aero, Blowers insisted that the firm was a generic charter flight outfit that had nothing to do with ferrying terrorism suspects around the globe. "We flew those planes domestically," he told the *Smithfield Herald*. "None of our guys have been overseas. . . . I really don't understand what all the commotion is about."[3] When the *New York Times* followed up on the *60 Minutes* piece, however, Blowers acknowledged a connection to the government: "We've been doing business with the government for a long time, and one of the reasons is, we don't talk about it."[4] By 2006, Blowers had stopped speaking to the media entirely. "Enough has been stirred up already," said Lamar Armstrong, the company's lawyer, declining our requests for an interview.

But Blowers' repeated insistence that his company is a run-of-the-mill aircraft charter company is strongly contradicted by Aero's corporate records, by documents on file with the Federal Aviation Administration, and by stories told by ex-pilots. For example, in a November 30, 2001, letter from the FAA's registration file on the 737 Boeing Business Jet—the plane that ferried Khalid El-Masri, Binyam Mohammed, and countless others through the CIA's network of torture chambers and black sites—Blowers wrote to the Federal Aviation Administration asking that a registration number be assigned to Premier Executive Transport Services.

Maintenance documents from the Guantánamo Bay Express also have Blower's fingerprints on them: In a January 2005 letter to the FAA, Blowers wrote that "the registration number on the G-V *we operate* has changed to N44982" (italics added). Other letters and documents in FAA files reiterate the fact that Aero operates a number of the CIA's aircraft.[5] And information discovered in FAA records is corroborated, like so many other pieces of evidence, by the airplanes' flight logs. Whether the Guantánamo Bay Express flew some hapless prisoner to Kabul, or whether it shuttled dignitaries from foreign intelligence services to meetings in Washington, flight logs always show the torture planes coming home to Smithfield.

The problem with Bob Blowers' attempts at "plausible deniability" is that his version of "deniability" simply isn't plausible.

*   *   *

Aero Contractors is only one of the more recent incarnations in the history of the CIA's secret airlines. The agency has indeed controlled aircraft outfits for almost as long as it has existed. It started with a company called Civil Air Transport (CAT), formed in 1946 by Claire Chennault, Whiting Willauer, and Thomas G. Corcoran. Their intention was to use the company to support the Chinese Nationalists as civil war began breaking out in China. Chennault was a retired American general with a long history in China; he'd led the Flying Tigers (American volunteer pilots fighting on behalf of the Chinese against the Japanese) and the Fourteenth Air Force during the Second World War. CAT earned its money primarily from supporting nationalist Chinese paramilitary operations. In its first few years, CAT flew troops, supplies, diplomats, and other missions on behalf of Chiang Kai-shek's retreating forces. By 1949, however, CAT had begun to implode, squeezed from one side by the nationalists' diminishing fortunes, and from the other by crushing inflation in the Chinese economy. To sustain the company, Chennault proposed to the State Department that it begin to support nationalist forces in southern China and provide assistance to Chinese guerilla forces. Cennault calculated that the infusion of American dollars would help keep his company afloat.

But when the State Department rebuffed Chennault's plan, his business partner, Thomas Corcoran, put him in touch with the CIA's Office of Policy Coordination, whose deliberately vague moniker concealed its function as the CIA's covert-action arm. Frustrated by having to rely on American and British military air power for its operations, the CIA saw huge potential in controlling its own air assets, and on November 1, 1949, Corcoran signed a deal with the agency. CAT got $500,000 to finance a new base in Thailand and to relocate its headquarters to Hong Kong; it also received a $200,000 advance in exchange for giving the CIA priority access to the airline. The influx of CIA cash, however, didn't solve CAT's financial troubles, and after repeatedly going back to the agency for additional funds, the company was eventually absorbed by the CIA.[6]

Over the next decade, the CIA's growing paramilitary branch used CAT planes and pilots to expand its secret wars: first in China, then Korea, then in Vietnam at Dien Bien Phu. By the mid-1950s, CAT's operations had begun to spread around the globe in tandem with the CIA's increasingly global reach. In Central America, CAT cofounder Thomas Corcoran helped convince the CIA to wage a secret war against Guatemala's elected leader, Arbenz Guzmán. In addition to his role in CAT, Corcoran was also an employee of the agriculture giant United Fruit, a U.S.-based corporation with a firm grip on Central American agricultural exports. When Guzmán threatened to nationalize United Fruit's plantations, the CIA stepped in to put an end to Guzmán's "communism," and, in his place, propped up a series of brutal dictators.[7]

As CIA covert-action programs grew, so did the size of its fleet of "civilian" aircraft. In the late 1950s and early 1960s, the agency reformed CAT, turning it into the now-famous Air America. Air America eventually came to operate one of the largest fleets of civilian aircraft in the world, with 167 planes, 8,000 employees, and additional subsidiary companies dedicated entirely to maintaining Air America's fleet.[8]

Other CIA-controlled companies followed in Air America's footsteps: The agency bought a company called Southern Air Transport and operated it out of Florida,[9] and established another airline, Intermountain Aviation, in Marana, Arizona.[10] The names of these companies would become synonymous with secret wars around the world: Intermountain Aviation's name was attached to the assassination of Patrice Lumumba and the rise of arch-dictator Mobutu Sese Seko in the Congo; the name Air America was almost synonymous with the vast, semi-secret wars in Laos. And decades later, a reconfigured Southern Air Transport would become equated with the Reagan administration's illegal support for the Sandinistas, the Iran-Contra scandal, and persistent rumors of CIA drug-smuggling operations.[11]

The CIA's aircraft companies were almost shut down in the 1970s. After Congressional investigations led by Senator Frank Church and Representative Otis Pike revealed that the CIA had been involved in countless illegal activities, including spying on Americans, attempting to assassinate world leaders, and helping break into the Democratic offices at the Watergate Hotel, the agency was ordered, among other things, to sell off

Air America's planes one by one and, additionally, to sell off the entirety of Southern Air Transport.[12]

But the agency's air force would not be grounded for long. Instead of wholly owned CIA proprietaries like Air America, the CIA's changed tactics, getting airpower from a network of ostensibly independent charter companies who would maintain exclusive contracts with the agency. Aero Contractors, along with other companies like Summit Aviation, Corporate Air Services, St. Lucia Airwarys, and Tepper Aviation are the next-generation outfits, filling the void left after Air America's demise.[13]

*   *   *

To launch Aero Contractors, the CIA turned to a former Air America pilot named Jim Rhyne, a renowned figure in espionage circles who'd spent the 1960s and '70s flying planes for the agency, quietly moving men and materiel in and out of Southeast Asia during the Vietnam War. Rhyne had spearheaded Air America's operations in Laos, where he'd lost a leg during a firefight. For his contributions to the war effort, the Green Berets gave Rhyne an honorary beret, and the CIA awarded Rhyne the Intelligence Star and the Intelligence Cross, two of its highest honors.[14]

After successfully courting Rhyne to start Aero Contractors in 1979, the CIA directed him to find a low-profile airport no more than three hours flying time from Washington D.C., to serve as a home base. According to a former Aero pilot, who asked not to be identified, after Air America's dissolution, CIA higher-ups told

Rhyne that "We need to get this thing started up again. Go find us a location." Scouting for a site, "Jim just drove around looking at airports and facilities, looking for a place that would support our needs," recalled the former pilot. Rhyne was a Southerner, a Georgian, and he intended to base the new firm somewhere below the Mason-Dixon line. Smithfield met Rhyne's requirements: It was in the South, and it was reasonably close to Washington. Moreover, the airport was especially attractive because it had no control tower, which meant that the new company's operations wouldn't be vulnerable to wayward glances from airport staff.[15]

And indeed, until recently, the firm conducted its business with little scrutiny from Smithfield locals. "Nobody really dug too deep," the former pilot told us. "It's just a sleepy little town. I found it to be pretty backwards."

Much of the work the pilot performed for Aero was routine: "Ninety-nine percent of the flying was just hauling people around. It was really pretty mundane stuff... mainly in Central Asia and South America. We were on the transport end, the logistics aspect," he explained.[16]

But Aero Contractors' history, like that of other agency-controlled aircraft companies, is a history of covert operations and secret wars. During his time with the company, the pilot we spoke to helped the CIA carry out counter-narcotics raids in Latin America, usually flying twin-engine turboprop planes. He also flew in and out of Tajikistan in the 1990s, delivering agency operatives charged with recovering Stinger missiles from Afghan warlords. (After the Soviet Union withdrew from Afghanistan, the CIA sought to recover all Stinger missiles—a high-tech shoulder-fired device—it had distributed to the mujahedeen during the Soviet occupation.)

After 9/11, our source told us that Aero Contractors immediately doubled in size: "The company just plugged into a pipeline of cash. They went from thirteen pilots to twenty-five or thirty guys overnight.... They were flying people back and forth to Guantánamo."[17] With this influx of money, Aero expanded its fleet of planes. The company took control of several Spanish-made CASA turboprop cargo planes, which were registered to a front company called Devon Holding and Leasing, Inc. It also took control of the 737 Boeing Business Jet. Aero already controlled what would become the Gulfstream V Guantánamo Bay Express before 9/11.[18]

When it took possession of the 737 Boeing Business Jet, Aero was forced to expand its location to more than just Johnston County, because its home airport was too small to accommodate the 737. Aero promptly began building a twenty-thousand square-foot hangar at the Kinston Jetport in neighboring Wayne County, where the Business Jet would come to find its home.[19]

*   *   *

Revelations about Aero's involvement in the extraordinary rendition program have brought much unwanted attention to the county—"stirred up dirt," in the words of Aero's lawyer—but it would be an overstatement to say that revelations about

Aero's participation has caused a deep spiritual crisis in Johnston County. It's hard to know whether Smithfield's silence about Aero Contractors activities is prompted by fear, conformity, or genuine apathy.

When activists from North Carolina's Triangle region began protesting in Smithfield, Allyson and Walt Caison were some of the only local residents to join the protesters. But Allyson's decision to become active entailed more immediate ramifications for her place in the tight-knit community than it had for the protesters from out of town. "I feel like I'm really sticking my neck out because I'm a real estate agent," she told us. Her livelihood is dependent upon her reputation among her neighbors, many of whom work for Aero. Since she decided to stand against Aero, she and Walt have picketed the airport and communicated their anger to executives and board members. At a Holy Week Pilgrimage for Peace and Justice, a multiday, multicounty march, protesters carried wooden crosses and stopped at the airport to pray for the victims of CIA-sponsored torture, as well as for the souls of the torturers themselves. Allyson was the only county resident to participate. She carried a sign saying "AERO OUT OF JOHNSTON COUNTY."[20]

As we drove out of town, we were struck by how strange it is to be able to get so close to the rendition flights. Smithfield certainly isn't hard to find. And what goes on here certainly isn't much of a secret: It was all, we found, hidden in plain sight.

CHAPTER 3 *PLANESPOTTING*

We'll call him "Ray." He's asked that we not reveal his real name; he's simply not interested in having his identity known. We're driving just behind his SUV, and, after several hours on the road, we've finally come to a stop on a muddy dirt road just northeast of Sacramento in California's Central Valley, near the towns of Marysville and Yuba City. This is the California hinterlands. Ray has brought us here because nearby is a large chunk of restricted airspace, cordoned off for the exclusive use of Beale Air Force Base.

Ray is a planespotter—a person who's mildly obsessed with almost everything having to do with aviation. As a hobby, Ray tracks airplanes, logs their serial numbers and movements, analyzes their radio systems, and keeps detailed records of the frequencies and designs that their systems use. He tries to understand how aviation systems work, how planes communicate with the ground controllers and with each other, and how the military and the Federal Aviation Administration manage various kinds of airspace. On this mild spring day, Ray's testing a new piece of gear: a Kinetic Avionics SBS-1, a "virtual radar" system.

Attached to his laptop with a USB cable, the system allows him to watch air traffic within a forty-or fifty-mile radius and to log call signs and basic information about the planes.

Because Ray says that "tracking cargo and commercial aircraft near Oakland or San Francisco," where he's from, "is way too easy," our goal for the day is to work with Ray to track something a little more challenging: U-2 spy planes.

From our vantage point, we can see two of the infamous black spy planes circling lazily in the distance like giant condors. Ray fiddles with the gaggle of cables, antennae, rack-mounted radios, and the flashing LEDs of the electronic devices pouring out the hatchback of his SUV. Speakers sputter with the sound of military pilots periodically checking in with their control towers: "Dragon 73 on approach...."

"Dragon" is a popular call sign for the U-2, whose reputation for being difficult to fly has earned it the nickname "Dragon Lady."

On the screen of Ray's laptop is a list of all the planes that his "radar" sees—most are commercial flights: Alaska Airways, Southwest, and so on—and next to each identifying number is a call sign, a registration number, a country of origin, and an altitude indicator. At the bottom of the screen are a handful of numbers without registration information attached to them. These represent all of the military aircraft in the area. Some have call signs and some do not.

"REACH347 is probably a cargo-plane on an overseas flight," says Ray, referring to one of the military call signs, "as in 'reaching' across the ocean." He illustrates the call sign by extending his arm out toward the horizon as if he were placing a chess piece on the far side of a giant playing board. The call sign "GO DAWGS" is more ambiguous, although Ray surmises that it's some kind of inside joke—maybe a reference to the March Madness basketball tournament then going on. In the distance, a U-2 slowly climbs away from the base. On Ray's laptop, one of the unidentified planes' altitude numbers slowly keep time: 900 ft., 1,000ft....

"You're sure you see a U-2 ascending?" he asks us as he watches his screen. We answer yes, and then he writes down the number of the plane, filling in a small piece of the puzzle that the blank spots on the screen represent.

97

*   *   *

In Arthur Conan Doyle's first Sherlock Holmes novel, *A Study in Scarlet*, there is a scene wherein Watson studies an article over breakfast. When finished, he concludes that article's "reasoning was close and intense," but that its deductions were "far-fetched and exaggerated... 'From a drop of water,' said the writer, 'a logician could infer the possibility of an Atlantic or a Niagara without having seen or heard of one or the other."

Holmes, however, replies to Watson's criticism unambiguously: The conclusions are not far-fetched at all, for he knows that from a mosaic of seemingly disparate facts, a composite picture can easily begin to emerge.

Holmes's logic helps us understand how planespotters have helped unravel parts of the CIA's extraordinary rendition program. Planespotters were the first to notice the drops of water, which then helped others, armed with the planespotters' data, show the various structures of the CIA rendition program. Planespotters across the world watch thousands of planes, and their work documents some exceptionally ordinary facts. They know that airplanes land at airports, and they know that these airplanes can be identified by their tail numbers (which can change) and also by serial numbers (which do not). They also know that a civilian aircraft moving around the world leaves evidence of where it has been. There are geographical facts about where the plane was, and temporal facts about when it was in a particular place. Taken together, some of these seemingly inconsequential facts about airplane movements have gone a long way in documenting the activities of the CIA.

To be sure, planespotting might seem an eccentric hobby. Essentially, it is about paying attention to airplane traffic and keeping detailed records, or logs, of this traffic. There is satisfaction to be had from all this work and documentation; when the work is done, it's like successfully putting a puzzle together, solving a Rubik's Cube, or getting a high score in Tetris. It's about taking a seemingly chaotic set of circumstances (like air traffic at an airport), analyzing it, and appreciating the underlying order present in the system—"solving" the system. But unlike a cardboard puzzle, aviation systems are always changing, so the picture is never entirely complete. Effective planespotting takes extraordinary amounts of patience and extreme attention to even the most obscure details of a given system.

At the end of the day, planespotting is overwhelmingly about answering the "how" questions, as in, "How is air-traffic coordinated?" or "How does this undulating system adapt to changes over time?" For the most part, planespotting is decidedly *not* about asking the "what" and "why" questions, like, "What, exactly, does this mean?" or "Why is a given set of things happening?" An online planespotting forum is usually the wrong place to a find a discussion of "torture planes," even though these same forums can be treasure troves of information about them.

The tools of the planespotters' trade go from the tried-and-true to beyond-the-bleeding-edge. Most of the world's planespotters use nothing more sophisticated than a notebook and pencil, although a camera with a telephoto lens attached is a standard accessory. When a plane arrives or departs a given airport, the planespotter will write down the plane's tail number, owner, and the exact time of the event. If a particularly exciting plane comes through, he or she might take a picture. After a day's planespotting, the hobbyist might post their logs and images to a forum like Airliners.net or Planespotters.net. This is the tried-and-true approach to planespotting, and it works just fine.[1]

Taking planespotting to the next technological level means getting some radios involved, and there are a huge number of variations on this theme. The most basic level of radio-logging involves a scanner—a kind of radio that can pick up frequencies far above and below commercial AM and FM stations. A lot of the world runs on radio frequencies, and aircraft are no exception. Basic planespotting with a radio involves tuning to aviation frequencies and listening to traffic between pilots and ground controllers. By listening to air traffic, one can get much of the same information that someone at the airport with a pencil and notebook can get. In addition, one can analyze how the radio systems themselves work. People who do this kind of "monitoring" also post extensive logs to online forums.[2]

But radio methods aren't limited to eavesdropping on air traffic. The airwaves are filled with far more information than just voice traffic. Moving toward the advanced end of radio-planespotting, there's ACARS, an acronym for Aircraft Communication Addressing and Reporting System. Put simply, ACARS is like an automated email system used by aircraft and ground control. An ACARS-enabled plane will transmit all kinds of information about what the plane is doing: where it is and where it's going, how much fuel it has, what the weather is like, and so on. These automated "emails" between aircraft and their ground controllers are encoded into radio signals clustering around the 131 megahertz and 136 megahertz frequencies. A good scanner can receive these radio signals. To the ear, the transmissions sound like noise, but when attached to a computer equipped with a software-based decoder the information contained in the airplanes' messages becomes visible. Like notebooks filled with tail numbers and landing times, ACARS monitoring produces an endless stream of information for ridiculously detailed logs, which ACARS enthusiasts from around the world dutifully post online.[3] In 2004, a particularly colorful ACARS log made the rounds on planespotter listservs. It had been intercepted by an ACARS enthusiast in the Netherlands, and had been transmitted from a Gulfstream Jet owned by Braxton Management Services and operated by Centurion Aviation—a possible CIA flight:

```
(2AAAEN50588E 5067DISPATCH N478GS CAVM

WHAT.S.UP.WE.HAVN.T.HEARD.FROM.YOU.TODAY.DON.T.YOU.

LOVE.US.ANYMORE.WE.ONLY.BEEN.GONE.2.DAYS.AND.YOU.

ALREADY.FOUND.SOMEONE.ELSE.)[4]
```

As complicated and powerful as ACARS-logging seems, there's another vastly more powerful technique at the far end of the planespotting spectrum: the data feeds.

Every subculture has its treasured secrets, whether it's the location of an obscure pressure-point among martial artists, or a "magic bullet" ball among golfers. In planespotting circles, the trade secret takes the form of the data feeds, a direct link with the Federal Aviation Administration's computers. Among the initiated, the data feeds have a quasi-mystical status: Almost no one will talk about it on listservs or public forums, and when someone posts data originally collected from the data feeds to an online forum, they'll usually try to find a second source for the data (like an ACARS log) in order to mask the information's true source.

The data feeds work like this: The Volpe National Transportation Systems Center in Cambridge, Massachusetts, (a division of the Department of Transportation) publishes a constant stream of information for all of the air traffic in and around the U.S., which is called the Enhanced Traffic Management System (ETMS). Air traffic controllers use the data to help coordinate air traffic and keep the skies safe. But numerous commercial ventures have also sprung up around the data—airlines publish data culled from the system on their websites, allowing people to check their flight status online. The data has numerous uses, from limousine companies making sure that their drivers are in the right places at the right times, to managers at charter aircraft companies paying attention to their own aircraft fleets.[5]

Planespotters can theoretically just type the tail numbers of planes they want to watch into a commercial service like Flight Aware and get all the ETMS data they want.

But there's a catch: Some of the more interesting planes, including many torture planes, are "blocked"—that is, they've been filtered out of the data feed at the plane owner's request. In many cases, however, the "block" request doesn't go directly to the source of the data, but goes, instead, to the commercial providers (like Flight Aware), who are in turn expected to ensure that end-users (like a curious planespotter) can't see these blocked aircraft.

However, as any thirteen-year-old computer programmer will tell you, where there's software, there's a hack. There's no video game protection, no DVD encryption scheme, no firewall, or copy-protection algorithm that someone, somewhere, hasn't figured out how to hack. And in the information age, attempts to block the flow of digital data, whether it's copy-protected movies or flight logs, are practically invitations to a hacking contest.[6]

The data-feed technique isn't one singular approach—it isn't some kind of "all-in-one" master planespotting solution. Navigating the data feeds means knowing how various commercial providers interpret the raw data, knowing what each piece of software is good at doing, knowing where to locate various glitches and hacks to show the blocked planes, and knowing how to apply and use them. Planespotters who really know their way around the various services might be able to see military planes and torture planes and then monitor these planes' landing at noteworthy airstrips. By accessing multiple sources of data, one can find bits and pieces of raw information, and these bits and pieces of information can provide the Holmesian drops of water that one might use to infer the existence of oceans.

103

*   *   *

Ray is somewhat unique among planespotters because, much more than others with the same hobby, he tends to move beyond the "How does it work?" questions and venture into "What does it all mean?" When he logs new aircraft or sees suspicious movements, he's quick to check newspapers and, when necessary, file

Freedom of Information Act requests to develop a deeper understanding of what he's logged. Because he follows up his planespotting with intensive database and Internet searches, phone calls to journalists and public-affairs officers at military bases and airports, he's made some discoveries about the workings of the U.S. military and other government agencies that add up to much more than a sum of collected data. That's how he inadvertently discovered the torture planes. He became aware of the network of unmarked airplanes, front companies, and unexplained incidents involving American "civilians" around the world after noticing a collection of unusual aircraft at a remote airstrip in central Nevada called Base Camp. "If you want to know about how I started tracking these torture planes," Ray would later explain to us, "I think we're going to have to talk about Base Camp."[7]

Base Camp is about ten miles northeast of Warm Springs at the junction of Highway 6 and Highway 395 in Nevada's remote Hot Creek Valley. Base Camp is little more than a dusty collection of trailers with an adjacent airstrip. It's an active, albeit small, installation, and no one quite knows for sure what goes on there. The facility was originally built in the late 1960s to house Project Faultless, an exploratory effort to move underground nuclear testing away from the Nevada Test Site. (Las Vegas casinos had begun to complain about the earth-trembling explosions just to their north.) After a particularly disruptive January 1969 test at the Faultless headquarters, the Atomic Energy Commission deemed this part of Nevada unsuitable for further nuclear testing and closed shop at Base Camp. Years later, however, the Air Force claimed Base Camp for its own operations, withdrawing six hundred acres of public land for a "communication site and support facilities,"[8] and proceeded to build a 7,300-foot runway and install air-navigation equipment at the site. Although the Air Force has run Base Camp for more than twenty years, it remains unclear what the Air Force does there.

And this is why Base Camp is so interesting to planespotters. Base Camp looks characteristically like a secret military base. First, the runway has large "Xs" painted on either end, a mark that usually means an airfield has been decommissioned or is otherwise unsafe for landing. This is unusual, because Base Camp is clearly an active installation, no matter how small or secret. Second, there have been persistent rumors that Base Camp is somehow connected to the "non-existent" Area 51 base to the south—serving as an emergency landing strip for experimental aircraft, as an isolated testing area for people working on projects so secret that they aren't allowed into public places, or for unknown support activities related to other military sites in the vast expanses of central Nevada. Unmarked passenger planes that have been spotted flying into Area 51 have also been seen at Base Camp.

One day in late 2001, around the time that Binyam Mohammed was abducted from Karachi, Pakistan, in a Premier Executive Transport Services Gulfstream, Ray was driving from a favorite lookout site near the town on Tonopah, Nevada, to another desert lookout almost a hundred miles to the south. Base Camp wasn't too far out of the way, so he decided to make a short detour past the installation on the off chance that something was going on. As Ray approached the airfield in his dusty 4x4, he almost crashed his truck when he saw what was happening. There on the tarmac were a total of four unmarked aircraft—and he didn't recognize several of the models. Ray decided to play it cool and quietly drove past the collection of planes and a small crowd of people in civilian clothes clustered around them who appeared to be refueling the planes. When he was out of sight, Ray pulled over, attached a telephoto lens to his camera, and loaded it with a fresh roll of Fuji slide film. Ray then turned his truck back around toward Base Camp, stopped near the fence line, opened the car door, and "click, click, click, click—I got all the tail numbers, then put on a 55mm lens to get a group photo. Around then, I realized that they were watching me, so I got back in the car and high-tailed it out of there."[9]

Later that night, from a desert motel near the town of Caliente, Ray posted his findings to an online forum. "There were four planes at Base Camp today," he wrote, "which is exactly four more planes than I ever saw there before."

Two of the planes, a Pilatus PC-6 Porter and a Construcciones Aeronáuticas S.A. (aka CASA) CN-235 had military serial numbers: 56039 and 66049. The "civilian" Cessnas had the tail numbers N403VP and N208NN. A quick search of an FAA registration database showed that the two "civilian" planes were owned by a company called One Leasing, a company that Ray initially described as "an investigative dead end."[10]

Within a couple of hours of Ray's post, his listserv started crackling with excitement. "Guys, we are onto something here," posted one person to a popular listserv. "I just did a Yahoo search on '3511 Silverside 105' [One Leasing's published address] and found DOZENS of different companies at that same address and suite #. Look for yourself. What is going on here??!"

The planespotters initially assumed that the collection of aircraft had something to do with Area 51 (Base Camp was, after all, a "black site"). Could it be a crash-recovery team for some kind of classified aircraft?[11] But over the next few days, someone wrote that they'd spotted these same planes at North Carolina's Camp Mackall Army Air Field, home of the Delta Force and other Special Operations groups. Someone else discovered that the Base Camp planes were assigned to the USAF 427th Special Operations Squadron at Pope Air Force Base, which reported to the Air Force Special Operations Command at Hurlburt Field, Florida. Other planes from this squadron had been detached to Incirlik, Turkey, since the early 1990s and were suspected of flying missions into northern Iraq. The collection of planes spotted at Base Camp started to look less like something to do with "black aircraft" at Area 51, and more like some kind of Special Forces, or even CIA, operation in progress.

A few months later, Ray learned through "back channels" that his post about the Base Camp planes had caused heads to

roll somewhere in the shadowy world of military "black ops."
Apparently, someone, somewhere, had lost a contract because of
Ray's photos. At a desert bar, one of his friends—a man with an
unspecified connection to Base Camp—warned him over beers
to "stop messing with those Base Camp guys or you'll wind up
dead in the desert with two bullets in the back of your head."

"Wouldn't one bullet be enough?" asked Ray.

Ray started thinking about what he'd seen at Base Camp,
and started to think that these planes' registration numbers
might be the kinds of water drops that oceans could be deduced
from. It became clear to him that One Leasing (the owner of the
Cessnas) was some kind of a front company, although none of
the planespotters had realized it at the time. (They had,
however, noted that the types of planes at Base Camp had been
popular with Air America.) Ray started to expand the scope of
his plane-watching to include suspicious-seeming civilian
aircraft in addition to the military aircraft that were his first
passion. He examined copies of the CALP (Civil Air Landing
Permits), an Army document that listed the names of all civilian
aircraft companies cleared to land at Army installations and the
names of the installations they're cleared to land at. From the
CALP, Ray compiled an index of obscure companies with
clearance to land wherever they wanted, including such sensitive
installations as Bucholz Army Airfield (on the South Pacific
island of Kwajalein, home of the Ronald Reagan Ballistic Missile
Defense Test Site) and Wake Army Airfield. Suspicious names

from the CALP included Richmor Aviation, Stevens Express Leasing, Tepper Aviation, Path Corporation, Rapid Air Trans, Aviation Specialties, Devon Holding and Leasing, Crowell Aviation, and Premier Executive Transport Services.[12]

In December of 2002, when one of the Cessnas he'd spotted at Base Camp (N403VP) showed up at the Desert Rock Airstrip (DRA) with three other "civilian" planes, the puzzle he'd discovered the previous year got even stranger. But the DRA sighting also reaffirmed many of his suspicions about what he had seen at Base Camp. Here again was N403VP, a plane that he knew was connected to some kind of "black" activities. It now appeared to be attached to three other aircraft. He started plugging the tail numbers of the other planes into the FAA registration database. N8183J, a modified Lockheed C-130 with STOL capabilities, was owned by Rapid Air Trans and operated by a company called Tepper Aviation. He'd seen both companies listed on the CALP. N313P was the 737 Boeing Business Jet owned by Premier Executive Transport Services, which was also on the CALP's list of "worldwide" clearances. The fourth plane, N85VM (a Gulfstream), remained a mystery, but he put it on his "watch list" anyway.

Ray started tracking down other aircraft owned by the companies on the CALP document. He discovered a second Premier Executive Transport Services plane (a Gulfstream) with the tail number N379P, and another Cessna owned by One Leasing, tail number N1116G. He also learned that the company One Leasing shared an address with a number of other suspicious companies, including Southern Transport, Inc., and JSZ Aviation LLC. It also turned out that two of the planes that landed at DRA had serious and long-standing ties to the CIA. Austrian planespotters noted that a plane owned by Tepper Aviation had crashed in Angola in November 1989. The plane owned by One Leasing, a Cesna, later made headlines when, in February 2003, it crashed in Columbia. Revolutionary Armed Forces of Colombia (FARC) guerillas executed a passenger and the plane's American pilot.

When he put all these aircraft onto his watch list and started collecting information about their movements, Ray saw Premier's planes shuttling to and from Guantánamo Bay, Cuba, home of the notorious extraterritorial prison. The other Gulfstream, N85VM, however, was more of an enigma. It was owned by "Assembly Point Aviation," an aviation business owned by one of the Boston Red Sox's co-owners, but it was also a frequent visitor to Guantánamo Bay. Ray's logs started looking like this:

N85VM — ASSEMBLY POINT AVIATION (Operated by Richmor Aviation)

12/16/2002	OXC > IAD	(Oxford, Connecticut, to Dulles, Washington D.C.)
12/20/2002	KIAD > MUGM	(Dulles, Washington D.C., to Guantánamo Bay, Cuba)
12/20/2002	MUGM > KIAD	(Guantánamo Bay, Cuba, to Dulles, Washington D.C.)
12/20/2002	IAD > SWF	(Dulles, Washington D.C., to Hudson, New York)
12/23/2002	SWF > SCH	(Hudson, New York, to Schenectady, New York)

The plane seemed to be doing double duty, alternating between flying Red Sox luminaries around and making trips to places like Morocco, Romania, Qatar, and Guantánamo Bay. Ray later recalled, "When I saw them flying to Guantánamo Bay, that's when I realized these things were the real deal."

Ray wasn't alone—planespotters around the world were also beginning to notice these unusual planes and beginning to see entirely unpredicted connections between various unmarked aircraft and suspicious events around the world. The Internet was making it far easier to track aircraft and to share information with other planespotters around the world, and the Bush administration's "war on terror," now in full-swing, was providing plenty of suspicious activities to monitor.

111

*   *   *

In a small office at the headquarters of Human Rights Watch on the thirty-fourth floor of the Empire State Building in New York City, researcher John Sifton grabs a pencil and rummages around for a blank piece of paper. He then draws a crude map of the world and starts drawing lines across it. A straight line connects Kabul to Rabat, Morocco; another one connects Frankfurt, Germany, to Washington D.C. Sifton is trim, with blond hair and the unshaven face of someone who's been up for too many nights. He speaks with the combination of vitriol and confidence that's an unwritten job requirement for people in his business. As a terrorism and counterterrorism researcher, Sifton's duties include investigating and exposing the most egregious excesses of the United States' "war on terror." His job is to combine the skills of an investigative journalist with those of an unwavering advocate.

He is showing us how, by tracking CIA flights, he was able to learn of secret CIA prisons. In November 2005 editors at the *Washington Post* backed down under CIA pressure and declined to publish the names of two "European democracies" suspected of housing these facilities, but Sifton immediately cranked out a report fingering Poland and Romania by name. Sifton and the *Post* had independently reached the same conclusions, but it was Sifton who named the names. In his hands, flights logs begin to tell a long and complicated story. With his quickly drawn map, he's explaining to us how he's also been able piece together indications that the United States has had the help of numerous foreign countries in its "war on terror" and in its extraordinary rendition program. Just as maps of telecommunications systems or shipping routes indicate intricate webs of connection and collaboration between the world's businesses and governments, flight patterns and logs show similar international links and established relationships. And if maps of international telecommunication systems, financial networks, or shipping routes strongly suggest the economic and cultural phenomena that are often described as "globalization," then the flight logs of the torture planes, describing similar connections between unlikely locales, suggest another kind of globalization: a dark underside to globalization complete with hidden mechanisms of transnational coercion and control.

Whereas most planespotters only take their investigations so far, Sifton was and is looking seriously at the specific destinations of the rendition flights. In doing so, he has helped expose secret CIA prisons, but he is also keeping a watchful eye on the ever-changing roster of torture planes. "What I'm interested in are flights that aren't clear refueling stops along the way from one country to another," says Sifton after recounting the flight paths of several well-known rendition flights. "It's a simple question of geometry. This kind of flight," he explains while drawing a relatively straight line from Germany to Ireland to the United States, "isn't that interesting to us."

"What becomes interesting is anything which is—what do they say in geometry? Acute. Any kind of acute angle between arrival and departure becomes interesting to us because it suggests that the stop was a *destination*. A place you wanted to go." Sifton draws a line from the Middle East to Germany to Poland, an acute angle: "We were especially interested in airports that were not large, public airports.... Frankfurt is not even close to being a suitable candidate for an extremely sensitive clandestine CIA detention operation. By contrast, a small rural airport which isn't even open for regular civilian transport such as Szymany airport [in Poland] becomes suspicious, especially because it appears to be a destination."

A military airfield on the eastern coast of Romania, Mihail Kogalniceanu, also drew Sifton's attention for the same reasons. The Mihail Kogalniceanu airfield, just north of Constanta, has been used by the United States since 2002 for operations in

Afghanistan and in Iraq. The base had been closed to journalists and the public since early 2004. Donald Rumsfeld had visited in October 2004. It was suspicious.[13]

There were other things about Poland and Romania that stood out to Sifton. Flight logs would show a plane landing one place in either country, then taking off from a different place only minutes later. These sorts of little glitches and inconsistencies in the records didn't occur in other places. Other flight logs showed direct flights from Kabul to the Romanian cities of Bucharest and Timisoara, Romania, and to the aforementioned Szymany, Poland. Sifton started making calls to officials in Poland and Romania, trying to figure out what might be going on. "As we made inquiries, we got what I like to call 'reverberations'—a sense that something is going on. You'd ask people something and they'd respond in such a way that made you think something was going on. Not proof of anything, but it kept our interest." He eventually got to the point where the information was good enough to make a public allegation.[14]

As planespotters have long done, Sifton learned how to read the flight logs of known torture planes, following where they departed, arrived, and stopped along the way. As Sifton and other researchers learned, flight logs became much more convincing when they could be corroborated with other pieces of evidence. When multiple sources of information "reverberated" together, researchers could put together a convincing mosaic from bits and pieces of fragmentary information. Flight logs implicating

Poland and Romania as potential locations of black sites, for example, were corroborated by the testimony of three Yemeni men who the United States held incommunicado for more than eighteen months at a series of secret prisons in what appear to be at least three different countries.

Mohammed Faraj Bashmilah and Salah Nasir Salim 'Ali Qaru were arrested in Jordan and turned over to the United States in October of 2003. After being released in Yemen in March 2006, they provided stories that are among the very few accounts from people who have been held at the Eastern European black sites and released. When Amnesty International interviewed these men, they could provide little information about the locations of the countries where they'd been held, but their accounts of flight times and the conditions of the prisons made some strong suggestions.[15] Like others, Bashmilah and Salim were first taken to Afghanistan on a flight from Jordan that lasted about four hours. They knew that the prison in Afghanistan where they were held was run exclusively by Americans, and the men later said that they'd been held with a number of "important, high-ranking" prisoners, one of whom managed to tell them that he had not been held permanently at any one location and had been transferred with the rest of the group from place to place.[16] Each prisoner was held in complete isolation in a 6'x12' cell. Two surveillance cameras were installed on either side of the cell, and the prisoners were permanently chained to a ring fixed in the floor by chain that was not long enough to allow the prisoners to reach the door. Prisoners were taken outside for twenty minutes once a week, when they were brought into a courtyard and made to sit in a chair facing a wall.[17]

Toward the end of April of 2004, the men were prepared for transfer to another prison. They described a procedure similar to that of other rendition victims' accounts: They were stripped, put in diapers and overalls, then handcuffed, blindfolded, put in a face mask, had earplugs inserted into their ears, and were hooded with earphones over their hoods. Like the stories recounted by Binyam Mohammed and Swedish airport officials, the whole operation was conduced quickly and professionally by a team of black-clad and masked Americans.[18]

After several hours, Bashmilah and Salim's plane landed. They were then thrown into a helicopter with a dozen or more other prisoners. The helicopter flew approximately two and a half to three hours before landing, at which point the men were put in a car and taken to the black site. The car ride was between ten and fifteen minutes away from the helicopter's landing site along a bumpy road. When they got out of the car, the men were led up a flight of stairs, then into the building and down a ramp or slope. The walls were freshly painted, the toilets were modern, and the prison was highly organized and well-staffed.

There were a number of indications that they were in Eastern Europe, or at least not in a Muslim country. The toilets faced in the direction of Mecca (the direction of which they had been given for prayers). The hours of daylight fluctuated over the year, with sundown coming between 4:30 p.m. and 8:45 p.m., indicating that they were above the 41st parallel, significantly north of the Middle East. In the winter, they described being extremely cold, colder than anything the men had experienced. The food was also foreign to the men. The Americans served them food that they described as "European"—slices of bread, rice with canned meat, yogurt, and salad. On one occasion, they were served pizza, which they had never eaten before. On Fridays, Americans served the men Kit Kat bars.[19]

The Yemeni men's account of the facility seemed consistent with a report from Brian Ross of *ABC News* in which an unnamed source described a secret prison in Poland that had held at least twelve "high-value" prisoners in 2005, but which was shut down after Human Rights Watch named Poland as a suspected host of agency black sites. The source told *ABC News* that at secret facilities in Eastern Europe, Abu Zubaydah and others were fed "yogurt and fruit," "steamed vegetables and beans," and "meat or chicken and more vegetables and rice." Abu Zubaydah, said the source, was particularly partial to the Kit Kats given to cooperative prisoners.[20] Brian Ross had gotten confirmation from sources in the CIA that there had indeed been a black site in Poland starting in 2002, where at least twelve "high-value" prisoners were held. Eleven of these prisoners had been repeatedly and regularly tortured with "waterboarding." The exception, Ross reported, was Ramzi bin al-Shibh—a senior 9/11 plotter—who broke down crying and became cooperative after CIA agents showed him Khalid Sheik Mohammed's condition. Ross went on to report that although the site in Poland was opened in 2002, a second site in Europe—in Romania—was later opened, and several of the prisoners from the Polish black site were taken there.[21] In May 2005, the United States Embassy in Yemen informed the Yemini government that it would be returning Bashmilah, Salim, and another Yemini named Mohammed al-Assad to the country. The United States provided no evidence against the men. After a seven-hour flight, the men were given to the Yemini government, who in turn held them in prison for nine months before finally releasing them on February 13, 2006.[22]

The subsequent testimony of Bashmilah and Salim to Amnesty International didn't come as a surprise to John Sifton at Human Rights Watch. By tracking the torture planes, he had already known where many of the people kidnapped by the CIA were being taken. Like Ray the planespotter, Sifton had learned how to turn an airplane flight into a very big story.

*   *   *

It is tempting to overestimate hobbyist planespotters' contribution to unmasking the extraordinary rendition program. There are precious few people involved in the activity that go to the lengths that people like Ray have to decode the movements of suspicious aircraft and to interpret the brute facts that planespotters can supply. But a more lasting contribution from planespotting communities comes from the vast databases of images and information that they've accumulated. In these databases, numerous photos of the torture planes can be found. Additionally, we can't forget that the basic techniques of planespotting, and even the idea that flight logs and traffic patterns can reveal hidden geographies, became powerful tools in the hands of journalists and human rights activists trying to decipher outlines of the extraordinary rendition program by monitoring the movements of the torture planes.

119

British journalist Stephen Grey was one of the first reporters to have this insight, and he began compiling a database of flight logs using reports from planespotting websites, data from the ETMS system, and from other sources in the aviation industry. "I started to analyze what I found in the logs," he told us from London, "and I found there was a definite link between the flights recorded in the logs, reports of renditions, and accounts of current and former prisoners." Grey used his database of flight logs to contribute reports to the *New York Times, Newsweek,* the *Guardian,* and other papers—the data corroborated stories when hard facts were almost impossible to come by.[23]

But there is one final point to be made about planespotting, which is that it has turned into a rather large annoyance for the CIA, a "scourge" in the words of the *Guardian*. After a while, it seemed as if every big operation the CIA undertook was documented, somehow, by planespotters, who, in the main, had very little idea what they were doing.

At the Son San Juan airport on the island of Mallorca, a planespotter and city planner named Josep Manchado, for instance, had taken a picture of the 737 Boeing Business Jet (N313P) on the tarmac on January 23, 2004. He assumed that some kind of American millionaire was in town and took a photo and posted it on a planespotting website on a whim.[24] To Manchado's surprise, the innocuous photo of the American Business Jet began drawing interest from all sorts of different places. Emails and phone calls started arriving from the United States and Sweden—people asking about the unmarked Business Jet he'd photographed. "They obviously weren't all planespotters because they were asking questions that people who know about planes don't ask," he told the *Guardian*.[25] Journalists and researchers had begun to realize that the plane was involved in the rendition program, and, using Manchado's photograph, they were able to convince airport officials in Skopje, Macedonia, to show them their aviation records from the day German citizen Khaled El-Masri claimed to have been abducted from Macedonia. The records showed that the 737 Boeing Business Jet had indeed filed a flight plan on January 23: Palma de Mallorca—Skopje, Macedonia—Baghdad, Iraq—Kabul, Afghanistan.[26] Further investigation by other researchers showed that there was even more to the flight plan—the actual "circuit" had been Larnaca, Cyprus—Rabat, Morocco—Kabul, Afghanistan—Algiers, Algeria—Palma de Mallorca—Skopje, Macedonia—Baghdad, Iraq—Kabul, Afghanistan—Timisoara,

Romania—Palma de Mallorca—Washington D.C. The landing in Rabat, Morocco occurred on the same day that Binyam Mohammed said he'd been taken to Kabul. Thus, the flight logs corroborated both Khaled El-Masri and Binyam Mohammed's stories.

The planespotter who had started this chain of events had no idea what he was doing by posting the photo online. He was just documenting the landing as part of his hobby. As a fellow plane spotter put it, "It's not the CIA bit that interests us. You don't even know who owns the plane when you take down the serial number.... You keep accurate logs, for your own records."[27]

CHAPTER 4 DARK PRISONS

As our Ariana Airlines jetliner descended into Kabul International Airport, we were struck by the fact that Kabul looks more like a vast and unconstrained settlement than a major city. No skyscrapers line the sky, no glass buildings shimmer with the glint of the sun. Smog and dust fill the valley. Simple adobe dwellings clutch their mountainside foundations. If we didn't know our destination, we might have guessed that we were about to land at a rural military landing strip, not the biggest airport in the country. Our glimpses of Kabul from the sky attested to the successive waves of unresolved warfare that have sculpted the city. The worn and eroded craters and bombed-out aircraft are a reminder of Gulbuddin Hekmatyar's continuous mortaring of the airport during the never-ending inter-warlord skirmishes of the pre-Taliban era. Warehouses and depots near the airport have fresh scars and blast holes from American bombs.

As we strode across the runway to the bunker-like terminal, a convoy of Humvees motored toward an idling Blackhawk helicopter, while, overhead, an F-16 lit its afterburner with a sky-splitting scream and thundered away.

Inside, the terminal was dirty and dark—half the lights were broken or flickering—and large chunks of the metal ceiling drooped precariously. Most of the signage was hand-written and the lone luggage carousel was only semifunctional. Painfully skinny Afghan police checked visas, while hefty white men in Oakleys and body armor toted Swiss-made submachine guns in the baggage area just beyond the last of the numerous checkpoints.

The airport, we would soon find out, was emblematic of the entire city: Five years after U.S. soldiers arrived, Kabul was still wrecked, still a combat zone. Throughout the city, electric power was intermittent. Every traffic light in this metropolis of three to four million was busted. Huge numbers of people were still dwelling in the rubble, squatting in bomb-collapsed buildings or camping beside the ruins of their obliterated homes. And the hostilities were ongoing, albeit on a decidedly smaller scale.

We'd come to Kabul to search for black sites, the secret CIA prisons where detainees from the war on terror are held incommunicado and tortured. From media reports and interviews with human rights experts, we'd learned that Kabul is, or had been, home to at least two of these facilities. The first, located in an old brick factory on the outskirts of town, was known by a code name: "the Salt Pit." The second facility had earned the nickname the "Dark Prison" or the "Prison of Darkness." We wanted to see these places, to see what kind of local knowledge Afghan people living around the facilities had and, if at all possible, to talk to people who'd been held in them.

At the time of our investigation in Afghanistan, very little was known about the "Dark Prison." Several prisoners held in CIA custody for several years before ending up at Guantánamo Bay had described the place, and they believed the Dark Prison to be situated in or around Kabul. No one besides the agency and its allies, however, is sure of exactly where the facility is located. Some theorize that it may actually be located on the same "campus" as the Salt Pit. Ex-prisoners, including Binyam Mohammed, Jamil el-Banna, and Hassan bin Attash, offer similar and consistent accounts of the Dark Prison: They describe a darkness so thick that they could not see their own hands; Eminem's *Slim Shady* album and other abrasive music and sounds were blasted twenty-four hours a day; interrogations were held under strobe lights; and prisoners were strapped to the ceiling. Bisher Al Rawi, who was held in the Dark Prison beginning in December of 2002, described "some sort of satanic worship music" in constant rotation, impenetrable darkness, and the unsettling sight of masked guards periodically moving through the corridors with dim flashlights.[1]

Although we made repeated inquiries about the Dark Prison while in Kabul, we focused our efforts on the Salt Pit, which we knew to be located near the Kabul airport. The *Washington Post* had disclosed the code name of the facility in March of 2005. At that time, the paper had reported that the facility had been "torn down" and relocated elsewhere. In November, the *Post* added, in its important report on the secret CIA secret prisons in

Eastern Europe, that problems with security on the road leading to the Salt Pit had caused the facility to be temporarily abandoned during the years of its operation. During the time the facility had been closed, the *Post* reported, prisoners had been moved inside Bagram airbase and, eventually, to another location.[2]

Once the *Post* disclosed the CIA code name "the Salt Pit," we began following the story. Immediately interesting to us was a current satellite photo of the Salt Pit that the *Post* had published with its November report; the photo showed two large structures. When we procured a second satellite photo, one taken in early 2001, it was immediately clear that the site the *Post* had disclosed was indeed in heavy use: The early photo showed only one building. The second building had been added after the American invasion.

Working with easily accessible satellite imaging services, we worked to confirm that the photo the *Post* had published was indeed the Salt Pit. Detainee accounts had all noted that the prison was only a ten-minute drive from an airport. Because we knew that the rendition flights landed at Kabul, we assumed, given driving conditions in Afghanistan, that the facility in question could not be more than four to six miles from the airport. Armed with a map drawn by former prisoner Khaled El-Masri, we were able to confirm that the facility the *Post* had highlighted must indeed be the Salt Pit. Because no journalist had ever visited the site, we wanted to see the facility up close.

*   *   *

Our home base for our time in Kabul was the Mustafa Hotel, a five-story, '70s-vintage structure in the center of the city that regularly plays host to low-budget foreign journalists, U.S. military contractors, and freelance soldier-of-fortune types. Guarded around the clock by burly AK-47-equipped security, the Mustafa also happens to be one of two places you can buy alcohol in Kabul. Among locals it's somewhat notorious for incidents like a gun battle that erupted in the lounge between two drunken Yanks—a GI and an ex-GI—that purportedly lasted three hours and consumed over one hundred rounds. The mirrored walls of the lounge were still pockmarked with bullet holes some six months after the firefight.

Locals call the Salt Pit the *Hecht Hochtief,* recalling the German construction company that had built the factory before civil war had ripped the country apart. We asked our translator to find a driver familiar with the outskirts of Kabul to take us to the abandoned factory. "We need to find an old man," he had informed us. "Someone who has been in Kabul long enough to remember when the place was still a working factory." When we finally found a driver who knew the way, he asked for fifteen dollars, big money in Kabul.

As we slipped out of town, the already rutted road worsened, the dust thickened, and the air grew hotter and drier. There are two major roads that connect Bagram and Kabul, and this road is, by far, the less traveled. We quickly found ourselves in a desolate

The Salt Pit

valley, home only to a few scrap-metal yards. Plumes of black smoke rose from all around us—the product of brick-baking furnaces. (At one point along the way we encountered a bit of a traffic jam: a herd of goats pushed across the road by a bearded shepherd wearing traditional Afghan clothes, but, oddly, sporting a baseball hat. When the shepherd turned to look at us, we saw that his was a "KBR" cap—a gift, we supposed, from Kellogg, Brown and Root, the notorious military contractor and Halliburton subsidiary.)

As we approached the brick factory itself, we could easily confirm that the ten-acre campus, which is surrounded by a larger collection of structures and buildings, is still, in some ways, active. We knew from reports that some parts of the facility were used to train Afghan counterterrorist forces, with other parts of the campus used as a CIA substation. In CIA parlance, the Salt Pit was a so-called "host nation" facility—ostensibly run by Afghans, but entirely managed and financed by the CIA. (The *Post* had reported that the CIA pays the entire cost of maintaining the Salt Pit, "including food, water, and salaries for the guards.") It was important to the CIA that outsiders understood the compound to be a "host nation" facility. If, for example, a prisoner were beaten, tortured, or died in the hands of Afghan guards, the agency could either deny responsibility for the incident, or argue that the site wasn't under U.S. jurisdiction.[3] We were thus not surprised to find a large hand-painted sign at a checkpoint that labeled the facility, in English, as an Afghan military facility. NO PICTURES, it noted.

As we approached the facility, we looked beyond the wall and past the guard towers and saw the dilapidated ex-brick factory. It matched the satellite photos. We knew that it was *Hecht Hochtief*, the Salt Pit, but asked guards who stopped the car, and who were wearing unmarked green uniforms, what the place was. They predictably replied that it was an Afghan military facility.

We pressed them, asking if there were Americans there. The guard said: "Yes, lots of Americans." We observed two American sitting on a nearby Humvee.

We tried to informally ask other questions, but the guards, not responding, lazily asked where we were going. Realizing no more information was forthcoming, we replied, "Back to Kabul."

*   *   *

The origins of the Salt Pit lay in the U.S.-led war against the Taliban. When the American forces and the Northern Alliance captured prisoners on the battlefield they grouped them by their intelligence "value." Working in concert with the U.S. military and the Northern Alliance, the CIA sequestered "high-value" prisoners at Bagram Air Base, an Afghan installation that had been commandeered by American troops. The agency housed the inmates in a prison made out of shipping containers surrounded by a wire fence.[4] This makeshift facility served as the first black site. Meanwhile, warlords like General Abdul Rashid Dostum received "low-value" prisoners, holding them, in many cases, in shipping containers as well—and, at times, slaughtering them en masse.[5]

In late 2001, the agency abandoned the shipping containers of Bagram in favor of the crumbling brick factory not far from the base. The Salt Pit provided more permanent housing for the CIA's "high-value" prisoners.

Anonymous sources told the *Washington Post* that there weren't a lot of veteran CIA officers willing to volunteer for an assignment as the chief of the isolated prison and that the case officer in charge of the black site was a rookie and on his first assignment. It was a new kind of assignment for the CIA—running secret prisons was not something that the agency had historically done. In 2003, a prisoner froze to death after the young case officer in charge of the Salt Pit ordered the man stripped, chained to the concrete floor, and left overnight without blankets. The next morning, the prisoner—an Afghan in his twenties—was dead. After a CIA medic ruled the man's cause of death as "hypothermia," Afghan guards buried the man in an unmarked grave. His family was never told of his fate, and his remains were never returned home. In the spring of 2004, the CIA referred the case to the Justice Department for possible prosecution. The Justice Department came back with a decision not to prosecute the case: The Salt Pit, it ruled, was a foreign facility outside of its jurisdiction. The case officer was promoted.[6]

The most detailed account from within he Salt Pit comes from Khaled El-Masri, a Geman citizen of Lebanese descent, who was kidnapped by the CIA in January 2004 and held incommunicado for four months. He was grabbed while on vacation in Skopje, Macedonia, and detained in a Macedonian hotel, before a squad of masked Americans hustled him onto the 737 Boeing Business Jet owned by Premier Executive Transport Services and flew him to the Salt Pit, where he was subjected to treatment considered torture under international law. El-Masri was eventually released in Albania. His incredible tale stirred an international media storm.

In media interviews and sworn testimony, El-Masri recalled a ten-minute ride from the Kabul Airport, after which his masked captors pulled him down a flight of stairs into the recesses of a building. With their boots on his head and neck, the Americans removed his chains, took off the hood covering El-Masri's eyes, and left. After his eyes adjusted, El-Masri saw that he was in a makeshift prison cell.[7]

El-Masri described a cell in which bits of plaster and paint lay scattered over a dirty plastic carpet on the cell's floor. What passed for a bed was a mat made from filthy clothes topped with a thin military blanket. A plastic bottle filled with greenish-brown water stood in the corner of the room. The cell's walls were marked by bits of graffiti left from unknown prisoners who'd lived there before—there was writing in Arabic, Farsi (spoken in Iran, Afghanistan, and parts of Tajikistan), and Urdu (Pakistan's national language). He could make out verses from the Quran, aphorisms, and dates in the scrawl on his cell walls. When El-Masri looked out through a small window in the cell door, he saw a guard in Afghan clothes staring back at him.

"I signaled the Afghan that I wanted something to drink," he recalled of his first day in the Salt Pit. "I had never been that thirsty before in my life." The Afghan guard pointed to the bottle of putrid water in the cell's corner. "I thought he had misunderstood me and I tried to tell him again that I wanted water to drink," El-Masri remembered. The Afghan guard pointed once again to the stinking bottle in the corner—"He meant to tell me that either I drink this water or nothing, that there was only this water here for me to drink."[8]

On Khaled El-Masri's first night in the Salt Pit, four masked men in black uniforms arrived at his cell and dragged him to another room, where three masked men sat at a table. One of the masked men, who spoke to El-Masri in Arabic with a Palestinian accent, told the prisoner to remove all of his clothes for a medical examination. The men photographed El-Masri and took a blood and urine sample. When El-Masri complained about the water, he was told that "this wasn't their problem, but it was the Afghan's responsibility." The men then asked if El-Masri wanted Islamic or un-Islamic food while at the prison. After requesting Islamic food, El-Masri found out that it consisted of leftover skin and bones from the Afghan guards' meals. The masked men took him back to his cell, where he groped around in the unlit room for the tattered bed. "It was cold in Kabul at this time, and I only had one blanket."[9]

The second night, the masked men returned. They chained El-Masri's hands and feet and shoved him into an interrogation room. In the room were seven more men, all wearing the same matching black uniforms and masks. Another man, who spoke Arabic with a south Lebanese accent, started screaming that El-Masri "was in Afghanistan, where there are no laws, and that nobody knew I was here.... 'We can do with you whatever we want.'"[10]

*　　*　　*

We weren't just interested in staring at the compounds that held detainees—we wanted to actually talk to people who'd been held in the Salt Pit, Dark Prison, or any other secret facilities. To that end, we met with journalists of Pajhwok, one of the few independent news agencies in Afghanistan, a sort of Afghan Associated Press with twenty-three journalists spread across the country in ten different bureaus. We met Farida Nekzad, Pajhwok's managing editor, in the organization's backyard, on a tree-shaded stone patio surrounded by a high stone wall topped with spikes and defended by armed guards. Our hope was that Nekzad and her colleagues might be holding some clues about the CIA's secret facilities, or might have interviewed people who'd been jailed and released by the agency, or might know who we should talk to.

The first thing we had to do was specify that we were interested in prisons holding non-Afghans—specifically, people who'd been grabbed in other countries and brought to Kabul.

The clarification was important since the U.S. had captured plenty of foreign jihadis who'd been fighting alongside the Taliban. The people we wanted to know about were people like Khaled El-Masri, men who'd been abducted by the CIA and transported to Afghanistan so they could be questioned and tormented with impunity.

While extraordinary rendition had become a hugely contentious political issue back home—not to mention Europe, where the Council of Europe, as well as the governments of Germany, Italy, Spain, and Britain were investigating the subject—in Kabul, the apparent endpoint for many the renditions, there'd been little reportage or public discourse on the matter. Nekzad was unaware of El-Masri's lawsuit or the broader global furor over rendition.

"We haven't been able to get into the jails where the Americans keep prisoners from other countries," said Nekzad, who wore western clothes and bright, glittery, gold nail polish. "They have very tight security—and it's not Afghan security." In fact, Nekzad continued, she and her colleagues hadn't been able to visit any U.S. detention facilities—and neither had the Afghan government. But she'd heard about what might be another secret American jail, a place near Kabul's District 10 police station, not far from the Haji Yaqoub crossroads. Nekzad stressed that she was just going on whispers and speculation about the place. "We've heard there are foreign prisoners there, but we don't have any proof. We cannot say definitively that it's an American jail because they have very tight security."

Another Pajwok journalist joined us and offered some more thoughts about the various prisons in Afghanistan. "In this country," he said, "the commanders, the warlords have their own jails in their own homes. Sometimes these jails are underground. In Baghlan province the local warlord has a jail made of shipping containers. Two weeks ago a man was killed in the jail. The governors also keep people prisoner in their homes, and in shipping containers. The governor of a province in the south has a jail in the basement of his house."

Despite the chaotic, ad hoc nature of the Afgan justice system, Nekzad was annoyed by the notion of the U.S. importing prisoners into her country. "Why are [the prisoners] here if they haven't committed a crime in Afghanistan?" she asked. "Every country has its own rules and constitution. Why should these people be here? Maybe the Americans think there are no rules here, no constitution." She encouraged us to check out the spot near the Haji Yaqoub intersection.

* * *

It was our translator's idea: We'd simply ask the police what they knew about the secret facility that Nekzad had told us about.

And before long, we had arranged an audience with the district police chief, who spoke to us in his office, a grimy room painted white, gray, and tan, and adorned with a color photo of the Northern Alliance leader Ahmed Shah Massood who had been assassinated just days before 9/11. The police official, a gruff

The facility on Street Two

man who would only identify himself as Mr. Habibullah—given the security situation, many Afghans, even government officials, are fearful of giving their full names to the media—shared a few tidbits of information. "Even Afghan police are not allowed to go there," Habibullah told us from behind his large wooden desk. "Only Americans can go there—and not all Americans. Nobody knows what happens there."

We thanked Habibullah for his time, shook his hand, and excused ourselves. As we walked past the stench of an open-air trash dump, we decided to check the place for ourselves and headed up the street. A couple of blocks from the police station, the road, Street Two, ended abruptly, cut off by a wall of five-foot-tall concrete blast barriers, sand bags, and coils of razor wire. A skinny Afghan guard sat in front of the road block. Our translator asked him what he was doing. "It's an American operation. They do counternarcotics and counterterrorism work," the guard replied. We told him we wanted to speak to the boss and the Afghan guy turned around and looked at the next line of security, a pair of Nepalese Gurkhas sitting in a plywood guard shack overlooking the blast wall. Wearing Oakley shades and pointing American-made M-16 assault rifles at us, one of the Gurkhas spoke into a radio.

Soon a pair of guys who looked like Americans (they were white guys in T-shirts and tan fatigue pants) emerged from the complex. They were armed with pistols. Looking at their stringy, unwashed hair—far longer than regulation military length—and lack of uniforms, we figured they might be the U.S. Army Delta Force, whose members are known for refusing to hew to standard Army grooming protocol; CIA operatives; or mercenaries working for a private military firm. When one of the guys opened his mouth, we immediately knew they weren't Americans—he had a discernable accent. "Bosnian," he explained, before refusing to tell us who he was employed by or what they were doing. Another character swaggered out to talk to us, a tall, heavily muscled black man cradling an assault rifle. This guy was actually an American—"from Maryland"—but like the others, he wouldn't give us a clue about what he was doing or what his name was.

*   *   *

As we hunted for people who'd been kept in the secret prisons, we kept hearing about Dr. Rafiullah Bidar, the regional director for the Afghan Independent Human Rights Commission, and a man reputed to know as much about what's going on inside the U.S.'s Afghan detention centers as any civilian in the country. Bidar has debriefed scores of ex-prisoners captured by the U.S. Through our translator, we arranged an interview with Bidar.

Our translator was a little nervous about heading to Gardez, a dirt-road city of some three hundred thousand southeast of Kabul. "Going to Gardez is risky," he told us, looking just a tad spooked. Bad things have a way of happening out in the provinces. In 2004, Medecins Sans Frontieres, the French medical aid group, pulled out of Afghanistan after five of its personnel were slain for no discernable reason in the northwest region of Badghis. Back in the states, an American professor who'd done research in Gardez had informed us that things could "get hairy there quickly." The town was more conservative than Kabul and was reputedly a hub of Taliban-type activity.

In preparation for the trip, our translator laid down a rule: Everyone would wear traditional Afghan garb in an attempt to blend in more with the locals. And he would check in regularly with friends at the UN about the security situation on the roads.

The drive to Gardez took us through a vast moonscape of sand and rock punctuated by the occasional mud-brick village. Out on the plains, herders led their mangy camels alongside piles of stones slathered with red paint—a warning that they were walking next to live minefields. The road, freshly built by a Turkish company, was a smooth, fast blacktop with no speed limit and little signage. We made it to Bidar's office without incident; only later would we learn that a bomber had blasted the town of Logar shortly after we drove through it.

Bidar, a Soviet-educated political scientist, is a small man with a bald head, prominent, arched eyebrows, and a salt-and-pepper beard. Sitting in his office, Bidar told us the Kandahar and Gardez offices of the Human Rights Commission were spearheading the organization's probe of abuse within U.S. detention centers. "In 2005 we worked on 113 cases of complaints of abuse by coalition forces," he explained. "Eighty-five of those complaints were handled by the Gardez office," while the Kandahar branch dealt with the remainder.[11]

The commission, he explained, was wary of being used as a propaganda tool for anti-American elements within Afghanistan. "Americans are here to help us, to rescue us. But we want the Americans to respect the law. They have to respect human rights," Bidar said.[12] "In 2005, the Americans admitted they have twenty jails all over Afghanistan and five hundred detainees," he told us. "It was a good achievement for us to get them to admit this. Unfortunately, we were not allowed to go see these prisons. Finally, we decided to do interviews with detainees released from jails. They told us how they were tortured."[13]

Most of the ex-prisoners were villagers captured for being alleged Taliban or al-Qaeda sympathizers, though Bidar thought that most of them weren't involved in politics at all.

A middle-aged man named Allah Noor, a small-time merchant with a produce stand in the heart of town, had a typical story. He was grabbed by U.S. soldiers on a winter afternoon in late 2003. "When they entered my shop they asked an Afghan translator to tie my hands," Noor told us. "They wanted to know 'where the guns were.'" The troops, he explained, thought he was providing weapons to the local Taliban guerrillas—though, in fact, he had no arms.[14]

The soldiers blindfolded and hooded Noor before driving him to a nearby base. When the blinders were removed he was in a locked room surrounded by two Afghan translators, three Americans in civilian garb, and three Americans in military uniform. They stripped him naked and took photos from all sides. Some of the U.S. personnel began asking him questions through the translators, while others, Noor said, "started to beat me very badly. Then they forced me to sit in a position that was impossible."[15]

He stood up and demonstrated this for us by bending over at the knees like a baseball catcher and then thrusting his torso forward in an obviously uncomfortable position. The beating went on for three hours, before they "gave me only trousers and put me in a big dark room. It was the beginning of winter. The room was very cold and there were holes in the roof. The snow was falling on me. I had only one thin blanket. I was under the snow for days."[16]

The next day, soldiers attacked him with a snarling German shepherd. For days he wasn't given any food, or allowed to use the toilet, or allowed to pray. Eventually, they put a hood back on and took him to Bagram military base via chopper.[17] Since the CIA moved its prisoners out of Bagram and into the Salt Pit in 2001, the U.S. military has used the base as a key jail for suspected insurgents.

At Bagram, Noor was hooded, handcuffed, shackled at the ankles, and thrown into another room. "I realized there were other people in there because they were moaning. Then they started to beat us with punches and kicks." Again, a dog was loosed on them. When he was pulled out of this room, the soldiers made him run to an interrogation chamber while hooded, chained, and cuffed.[18]

After the first interrogation session he was given strict commands, instructed not to talk to soldiers, nor to other prisoners, or to even look at other prisoners. The abuses went on and on and on for about five months, until, with little explanation, Noor was set free by the U.S. and walked out of the prison. He had no idea who his fellow prisoners were—he hadn't been allowed to speak to them—or whether the men who'd worn street clothes while questioning him were agents of the CIA or another intelligence service.[19]

Gannat Gul, a thirty-eight-year-old veterinarian, had a similar story. But unlike Allah Noor, Gul had eventually been permitted to talk to his fellow inmates at Bagram, and he learned that he was part of an international cast. Among the prisoners, said Gul, were Iraqis, Iranians, Saudis, Yemenis, and Pakistanis—none of whom had been caught in Afghanistan. All of them, he told us, had been abducted outside of the country and brought to Bagram.[20]

Gul remembered one Iraqi, a man named Mahmood, who shared the circumstances of his abduction: "He said, 'My wife is from Indonesia. When the fighting started in Iraq we moved to Indonesia to get away from the war. Someone must have said I'm with Saddam and Al-Qaeda.'" Gul continued: "The Americans came and arrested him and took him directly to Afghanistan. For three years he was in a secret jail that no one knows about. Then they took him to Bagram prison." Neither Gul nor Mahmood knew the name of this secret prison.[21] Gul had in his possession a military document showing that he was incarcerated by the "Combined/Joint Task Force (CJTF-76)" at "Bagram Airfield" for about two and half years before he was freed in January 2005, one of eighty-one people let go in a mass release of prisoners.[22]

Gul was furious with the United States. He accused the soldiers who had arrested him of stealing his most valuable possessions—a camera, a tape recorder, binoculars, and two wrist watches—as well as a life savings of 350,000 Afghanis (about $7,100). "I was not Talib. I was not Al-Qaeda," Gul spat. "They only came to steal from me. In all the world there is no bigger thief than America. America is the cruelest. I have lost everything." Among the things he'd lost was his UN-funded job caring for goats and other farm animals.[23]

The more people we interviewed in Afghanistan, the more obvious it became: Questions specifically about CIA black sites made little sense—they were hopelessly naïve, attempting to make distinctions where none seemed in order. For a somebody like Allah Noor or Gannat Gul, black sites were indistinguishable from military prisons, which were in turn indistinguishable from informal prisons run by the United States' warlord allies, which were in turn indistinguishable from the American occupation itself. The whole country was, in many ways, a giant black site.

The U.S. never told the men's families where they were. They never charged them with a crime. They never even told them, why, exactly, they were being released, when they finally walked free. It was, in short, exactly the sort of treatment suffered by the people snatched by the CIA and hauled to Afghanistan. (And both Noor and Gul suspect that some of the people questioning them were, in fact, intelligence agents.)

It's easy to imagine that when the Americans came to Afghanistan, they must have seen what Augustus had seen in the

German forest, or what King Leopold had seen in the uncharted recesses of the Congo: a space beyond the recognizable world; a dark, lawless space; an incoherent, incomprehensible space. A space where anything could happen. And somehow, in turn, imagination became reality. The act of seeing a space where anything could happen helped create a space where anything would happen. Afghanistan became a space in the image of the improvised and irregular CIA and Special Forces units. A space without uniforms, where it's unclear who is working for whom. Where violence is like the architecture: ad hoc, informal.

Afghanistan, given these American perceptions, was almost destined to end up playing host to a Dark Prison, to become a place where people like Khaled El-Masri, Binyan Mohammed, and countless others could simply vanish off the face of the earth. "We are in Afghanistan, where there are no laws... nobody knows you are here," the interrogators had told El-Masri. "We can do with you whatever we want."

*   *   *

As our 727 lifted off Kabul's battered airstrip for a flight to Dubai, the plane once again provided a brief view of the city. The bombing and ruin were once again plain to see. But there was something else. At the far end of the tarmac, nestled behind a chainlink fence, was a Lockheed Hercules aircraft, a white turboprop plane with a single blue stripe down its fuselage. We'd seen this plane before: as an icon on a computer screen, and as a registration number in a flight log. It was, in fact, one of the four planes that had landed at Desert Rock Airstrip more than three years before. A few months before we traveled to Kabul, we had tracked it flying out of the U.S. on a path that went from Florida, to Fresno, California, to Honolulu, Hawaii, and on to Andersen Air Force base on the island of Guam. Then it had disappeared.

CHAPTER 5 *RENDITION NOW*

NEW YORK LIFE

Near the main complex of Fayetteville Regional Airport is a tree-lined enclave inhabited by an unusual aviation company. We've come here to investigate a local company called Centurion Aviation. It's not clear what Centurion does. It has all the trappings of a small aircraft charter company catering to high-dollar, low-profile clients. There's a private parking lot for its customers, a discreet hangar, and individualized service. We know that the company operates two expensive executive jets.

Fayetteville, North Carolina, however, isn't known for having an exclusive class of ultra-rich jetsetters, nor is it a hideout for sheepish celebrities. Fayetteville, rather, is home to the U.S. military's Special Forces community. At nearby Fort Bragg, the famous 82nd Airborne Division has its home base. The Joint Special Operations Command, which coordinates special operations across the entire U.S. military, is also headquartered at Fort Bragg. And there are more secretive units too, including the 1st Special Forces Operations Detachment, Delta Force, which is charged with counterterrorist operations outside the United States.

Indeed, Fayetteville is home to numerous irregular military units: the soldiers armed with special-issue weapons, irregular tactics, and unmarked black gear instead of uniforms.

But the two planes Centurion operates are not standard military fare. Both are Gulfstream G-IVs; one has the tail number N478GS, the other N475LC.

Centurion doesn't own these two airplanes: When we began researching these planes, both were owned by Braxton Management Services. Braxton Management Services, and the company's officers, which included Matthew Hallman, Larry Scheider, Gary Hopkins, and Gary Lonergan, used the address of Lonergan's law office in Alexandria, Virginia. The law firm specializes in estate planning.

Centurion is listed on the CALP, which means that the two executive jets that Centurion operates are authorized to land at military bases. (As mentioned earlier, the CALP is the document that served as an initial "Rosetta Stone" of CIA front companies. Centurion first appeared on the document in 2003.) Centurion also has an account with the Defense Energy Support Center to purchase jet fuel directly from the military.

Because of the unusual facts that surround Centurion Aviation—facts that "reverberate" with many aspects of the rendition program—we are suspicious of Centurion. One Centurion planes has, for sure, been involved in some suspicious activities. Planespotters in Iraq spotted the Braxton/Centurion Gulfstream N478GS on the tarmac of an Iraqi airport, and the plane drew more attention to itself when it crashed on December 6, 2004, while landing at Baneasa Airport in Bucharest, Romania. According to the accident report, there were no injuries to the "three flight crewmembers and the seven passengers."

When Human Rights Watch revealed the following year that Romania was suspected of hosting a CIA black site in the vicinity of Bucharest, the crash of N478GS took on new meaning, even though there was no direct evidence of a connection between the flight, the CIA, and the suspected black site in Romania. Rather, at the time, there remained only a constellation of places, actors, and events surrounding Centurion that suggested a link between the company and some of the more irregular corners of the CIA, the Department of Defense, or "Other Government Agencies."

We are interested in Centurion because many of the planes we have been following have been sold off or grounded. The program is in constant flux: The airplanes being used, the locations of secret prisons, and perhaps even the identities of the governmental agencies involved are not fixed and can change quickly. As the details of a particular part of the program become public, someone, somewhere, changes them.

When we step back from investigating Centurion, it seems likely to us that the two planes operated by Centurion are part of a new generation of front companies. Like all fronts, however, Centurion's design is obviously intended to deliberately thwart any kind of rational analysis—companies like Centurion are built through secrecy, misinformation, and denials in such a way as to prevent any kind of irrefutable truth about the company from emerging. In the end, we want to say that Centurion is involved but, despite much investigation, we leave Fayetteville lacking unassailable proof.

*   *   *

After Swedish journalist Frank Laurin's exposé on the kidnapping of Ahmed Agiza and Mohammed Zery implicated the Gulfstream N379P, the Guantánamo Bay Express, and Premier Executive Transport Services in the extraordinary rendition program, other journalists began investigating the mysterious airplanes. These torture planes become open secrets: Planespotting forums reverberated with the tail numbers of the Gulfstream and Premier's 737, and bloggers devoted long pages to the planes' movements. And then something remarkable happened: Premier sold its two aircraft and appeared to close up shop.

November 10, 2004, saw a nonexistent person named "James J. Kershaw" sign a bill of sale transferring ownership of Premier's 737 Boeing Business Jet to an obscure company in Reno, Nevada, named Keeler and Tate Management, LLC. Six days later, "Kershaw" signed over the now-infamous Guantánamo Bay Express to a company in Portland, Oregon, called Bayard Foreign Marketing, LLC. "Tyler E. Tate" and "Leonard T. Bayard," respectively, took possession of the aircraft for the new companies, and within days of each other both "Tate" and "Bayard" both immediately applied to the Federal Aviation Administration to have the tail numbers of their respective aircraft changed: The Gulfstream became N44982; the Business Jet became N4476S. Like "Colleen Bornt" and "James J. Kershaw" before them, the names "Tyler E. Tate" and "Leonard T. Bayard" don't appear anywhere else in the public record.[1]

Both of these newly activated front companies had been set up in 2003, then left dormant until the agency needed them in late 2004. Bayard Foreign Marketing's corporate documents described the company as an "international marketing firm" located in Suite 755 of the Pittock Building in downtown Portland. Lawyer Scott D. Caplan, of the law firm Jordan, Caplan, Paul & Etter, played the same role for Bayard that Dean Plakias played for Premier Executive Transport Services: He filed their paperwork and lent his office address to the paper company.

Unlike some of the other front companies, however, Bayard had its own telephone number and address. The address attached to the number tracked back to a seemingly empty home in northeast Portland. When John Crewdson from the *Chicago Tribune* called Bayard Foreign Marketing's phone number, however, he found an operator who answered the phone "Baynard Foreign Marketing." The operator claimed to have never heard of "Leonard T. Bayard." When Crewdson called back a few minutes later, a different person answered—this time, correctly, saying "Bayard Foreign Marketing," and claimed that "Mr. Bayard is away from his desk." Crewdson suspected that the phone was "back-stopped"—that is, that the local number in Portland was being secretly forwarded to operators at CIA headquarters in Langley.[2]

The second of the new front companies, "Keeler and Tate Management LLC" was also established in 2003, and was head-quartered at an address in Reno, Nevada. On a cold, gray December day, we paid a visit to the Nevada secretary of state's office, a little stone building in Carson City, a small town nestled between snow-flecked Sierra peaks. The office, which oversees all businesses incorporated in the state, has several documents related to Keeler and Tate on file.

According to the state records, Keeler and Tate is owned by Tyler Edward Tate, whose signature appears on three different official documents. The signatures vary markedly from docu-ment to document, and, there does not appear to be a Tyler Edward Tate anywhere near Reno. He's not in the white pages and the name didn't pop up in an extensive review of online databases. Tyler Edward Tate was another "sterile identity."

The only live person we could find on the Keeler and Tate paperwork was—as with the other front companies—a low-profile family lawyer who acted as the Keeler and Tate's registered agent. This one was named Steven F. Petersen, who runs his practice from a suite at 245 East Liberty St. in Reno; it's the same address listed on Keeler and Tate's official letterhead and is the only address listed on any document related to the company. We headed there next.

We got a surprise when we arrived at the building, a five-story brown-glass office cube in downtown Reno, a few blocks from the neon-lit casino strip. Petersen shares his suite with someone who has deep Washington D.C., connections, a man named Peter Laxalt.

Petersen and Peter Laxalt have a clear business relationship. The sign on the office door says Laxalt is "of counsel" to Petersen's law firm, meaning he works with Petersen.

The building directory says the suite is also home to the Reno branch of the Paul Laxalt Group, a major Capitol Hill lobbying firm.

A little background is in order: Peter and Paul Laxalt are brothers. A hawkish Republican, Paul Laxalt is one of the bigger names in Nevada politics, having served as governor, from 1967 to 1971, and later as a U.S. senator, from 1974 to 1987. He was a close confidant of Ronald Reagan (heading his election campaigns on three occasions), a strong supporter of the MX nuclear missile program, and a liaison between the Senate and the White House during the Iran-Contra scandal. An Army veteran, he was also, according to the *New York Times*, a good friend of late CIA director William Casey.

After leaving Congress, Paul Laxalt formed his lobbying firm, the Paul Laxalt Group, and hired his brother Peter.

We dropped by the office three times and confirmed that both Petersen and Peter Laxalt used the space, but we couldn't get past the receptionists, who, for some reason, didn't seem too concerned when we started talking about the CIA, torture, and mysterious aviation companies. Stymied, we placed a call to the D.C. headquarters of the Paul Laxalt Group, where we reached an employee named Tom Loranger, who told us, "We don't have an office in Reno.... I don't think Peter is working for us any more."

159

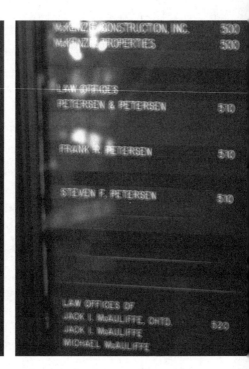

McKENZIE CONSTRUCTION, INC.	500
McKENZIE PROPERTIES	500
LAW OFFICES	
PETERSEN & PETERSEN	510
STEVEN F. PETERSEN	510
FRANK R. PETERSEN	510
PETER D. LAXALT OF COUNSEL	
PETER D. LAXALT, ATTORNEY	510
THE PAUL LAXALT GROUP WEST	
LAW OFFICE OF	
JACK I. McAULIFFE, CHTD.	520
JACK I. McAULIFFE	
MICHAEL McAULIFFE	

ABOVE: The building directory at 45 E. Liberty, Reno, Nevada

PAGES 160-161: Within days of the transfer of Premier's planes, an Irish activist-planespotter named Tim Hourigan wrote a bold headline for the Irish *Indymedia* website: "CIA Torture Jet sold in Attempted Cover Up." The connection between Keeler and Tate and Bayard Foreign Marketing Services, separate entities, can be seen quite easily in these two documents. Note that the registration number for Bayard's Gulfstream has been accidentally written, and then crossed out, on Keeler and Tate's letter.

Later, we called the office at 245 East Liberty one last time. The receptionist said we had indeed reached the Paul Laxalt Group, but, unfortunately, Peter Laxalt wasn't available. She took a message; he never called back.

After we reported the story for the *San Francisco Bay Guardian*, another remarkable thing happened: Journalists from the *Reno News and Review* paid a visit to 245 E. Liberty to follow up on our story, and found that the Laxalt Group's name had disappeared from the building directory.[3]

To the growing community of researchers interested in the extraordinary rendition program and the torture planes, the CIA's attempt to hide its trail behind new front companies and registration numbers was thoroughly transparent—researchers and planespotters know that an airplane's tail number and owner can change all the time, but that its serial numbers do not. Around the world, planespotters jockeyed to be the first person with a picture of the new tail numbers: "After the affair concerning its previous identity (N313P) was displayed by media..." wrote Mallorca-based planespotter Javier Rodriquez under a new picture of the Business Jet he shot in January 2005 and posted to the Airliners.net website, "[the plane] was quickly re-registered and 'sold' to an unknown company.... This is the first photo on the web in this registration."

But even as the planes began to receive unwanted widespread media scrutiny, their movements didn't stop. In the early months of 2005, the newly renumbered Business Jet logged flights to Tripoli-Mitgia, Libya, Baghdad, Iraq, Kandahar, Afghanistan,

161

Bayard Foreign Marketing, LLC
921 S.W. Washington Street
Portland, Oregon 97205
(503) 224-0417

November 8, 2004

44982 64
8068 V

10 DEC 01 2004

Federal Aviation Administration
Mike Monroney Aeronautical Center
Civil Aviation Registry, AFS-750
P.O. Box 25504
Oklahoma City, Oklahoma 73125

Dear Sirs:

Enclosed is the Bill of Sale and Aircraft Registration Application to register our newly acquired Gulfstream Aerospace G-V, serial number 581. The previous registration number was N8068V and N44982 has been requested and reserved.

Enclosed is a money order in the amount of fifteen dollars for the reserved tail number and registration.

Thank you for your attention in this matter.

Sincerely yours,

Leonard T. Bayard
~~Owner~~ Member

Enclosures as stated

Keeler and Tate Management Group, LLC
245 East Liberty Street, Suite 510
Reno, Nevada 89505
(702) 322-0673

November 10, 2004

$\frac{4476 \cancel{8}}{313P}$ 64

Federal Aviation Administration
Mike Monroney Aeronautical Center
Civil Aviation Registry, AFS-750
P.O. Box 25504
Oklahoma City, Oklahoma 73125

10 DEC 01 2004

Dear Sirs:

Enclosed is the Bill of Sale and Aircraft Registration Application to register our newly acquired Boeing 737-7BC, serial number 33010. The previous registration number was N313P and N4476S~~has~~ been requested ~~N4476S~~ and reserved.

N 4476 S

Also enclosed is one money order in the amount of $15 for the reserved tail number and registration.

Thank you for your attention in this matter.

Sincerely yours,

Tyler Edward Tate
~~Owner~~ *Member*

Enclosures as stated

and Khartoum, Sudan. For its part, the Gulfstream made flights to Bogota, Columbia, Cairo, Egypt, and numerous shuttles between cities within the United States.

But after the Human Rights Watch and the *Washington Post* published stories about "black sites" in Eastern Europe in November of 2005, there was far more media attention directed at these airplanes than their anonymous appearances could deflect. In December of 2005, the 737 Boeing Business Jet made a few local flights and settled into its hangar at Kinston Jetport in North Carolina to hide out for a while. In late January of 2006, it flew to Tuscon, Arizona, for a day and then returned to North Carolina. In June, it emerged again to visit Love Field in Dallas (where the plane had had maintenance done in the past) before returning once again to Kinston. Public attention, it seemed, had finally grounded the 737.

Aero Contractors continued to fly its small fleet of turboprop planes in and out of the country, but the telltale rendition routes became far less frequent. Through the chatter and gossip at church receptions and high school functions, Allyson Caison began hearing that her protests against Aero Contractors "were having an effect."

As for Aero Contractor's most famous plane, the Guantánamo Bay Express, the Gulfstream V with scores of rendition routes in its flight log, it showed up on the used-airplane market in December of 2005. The website of U.S. Aircraft Sales of McLean, Virginia, announced that it had the 1999 Gulfstream V (serial number 581) for sale. Apparently, there were no takers. Six months later, the airplane appeared on the market again, this time with colorful pictures of its refurbished interior.[4] The plane sported yet another new tail number: It seemed ironic that this aircraft, which had helped to disappear so many people out of existence, might now take on new life as a luxury transport, with a new interior that seemed designed to paint over the aircraft's haunted past.

Other parts of the extraordinary rendition program's infrastructure also began to disappear. In the aftermath of public accusations of black sites in Poland and Romania, the sites were quickly and quietly shut down. In the weeks between the news articles and Condoleezza Rice's visit to the continent, the CIA closed down the Eastern European prisons and arranged for the prisoners to be transferred to a new prison in the North African desert. When Condoleeza Rice visited a few weeks later, Poland and Romania would be able to say truthfully—in the present tense—that there were no secret U.S. prisons on their territory.[5]

*   *   *

At the headquarters of Human Right Watch, researcher John Sifton knew about the closing of the black sites in Poland and Romania. He also knew that there wasn't much activity from the 737 Business Jet and the Guantánamo Bay Express planes in November 2005. If the prisoners were transferred from Eastern Europe to North Africa in a civilian CIA plane, it wasn't either of these. Nonetheless, there was no shortage of suspicious planes fitting the profile of a CIA proprietary.

Planespotters in Frankfurt had become interested in a new Boeing Business Jet, painted white save for a green-and-yellow racing stripe down its fuselage, sporting the tail number N368CE. Its registration number led back to a Wells Fargo Bank (which could have either been the lease-holder or providing a cover). Like other suspicious planes before it, this Business Jet had also visited "lots of interesting places," including Nicaragua, Venezuela, Saudi Arabia, and Guantánamo Bay. By early 2006, planespotters had noticed that the plane seemed to be using Frankfurt am Main as a home base: "N368CE... Now a common sight in FRA, supposedly operating for the U.S. Air Force," wrote a planespotter on Airliners.net. Another commented that the plane supposedly flew for the CIA, but it didn't have any of the "special antennas" that other CIA planes seemed to have. On the other hand, the plane's routes had interesting timing: Beginning sometime around early 2006, it started frequenting Baghdad and Kabul, according to records various planespotters had acquired.[6]

But a central question remained: If the black sites in Romania and Poland were closed in late 2005, where is the black site in the North African desert where the prisoners were purportedly transferred? Despite official denials, strong "reverberations" have come out of Morocco. There are lots of signals, but they often contradict one another. A persistent rumor holds that the Moroccan secret police—the Direction de la Securité du Territoire (DST)—had provided a facility south of Temara, a rumor that corresponds to the testimony of Benyam Mohammed, who claims he was tortured in a Moroccan prison before being sent to the Dark Prison.[7] Flight logs examined by the Council of Europe show flight patterns between Washington, Guantánamo Bay, and the military airport at Sale, Morocco. There are also reports of a flight in early December 2005, when four blindfolded and handcuffed prisoners were seen at Sale coming off a 737 and whisked into a fleet of American cars, an event that would be consistent with other reports of prisoners transferred out of Eastern Europe before Condoleezza Rice arrived on the continent. When reporters from the *Sunday Times* visited Rabat in February of 2006, they found evidence of American involvement in the construction of a new DST prison at Ain Aouda near Rabat's diplomatic district.[8]

"Given all the chatter," says Sifton, "it would be difficult to maintain that 'there is not now and never has been any detention by the CIA in Morocco'.... It's just a matter of when and how and how many people."

*   *   *

The black sites, renditions, and the torture have not stopped. The details may have changed—the planes, the front companies, even the locations of the black sites—but the underlying structures of the program have not. Indeed, the counterterrorist program that the rendition program resides within has become, according to Dana Priest at the *Washington Post*, "the largest CIA covert action program since the height of the Cold War, expanding in size and ambition despite a growing outcry at home and abroad over its clandestine tactics." The overarching program has also acquired a code name, whose initials, GST, stand in for the classified name itself.[9]

With its origins in the September 17, 2001, memo granting George Tenet's "wish list" of new powers to the CIA, the GST program has grown to a tremendous size and shed the ad hoc qualities that it began with; it has become a dedicated bureaucracy. We now know that there are dozens of classified compartments within the GST program, including units responsible for mining financial records, eavesdropping on suspected terrorists, managing interrogations, coordinating efforts with foreign intelligence services, maintaining the network of secret prisons, and managing the fleet proprietary aircraft, among other activities. Workers in each compartment rarely have details about what their colleagues in other compartments are doing. Moreover, much of the debate about everything from interagency collaborations to interrogation techniques has become formalized in the CIA's Counterterrorist Center.[10]

We also now know that with the new organizational structure of GST, the CIA's capacity to kidnap suspected terrorists and consign them to an invisible world of secret prisons and torture grew exponentially. Ever-increasing numbers of tips and leads were the result of a growing intelligence collection effort, and, at the same time, expanded paramilitary capabilities meant that renditions became much easier for the CIA to pull off. Perhaps inevitably, however, standards for who would be kidnapped and held in the black sites became lowered: "They've got many, many more who don't reach any threshold," an intelligence official told the *Washington Post*.[11] Other intelligence officials said that the CIA inspector general was reviewing growing numbers of what they described as "erroneous renditions," dozens of cases in which the CIA had kidnapped the "wrong" person, or had kidnapped someone under distressingly low standards of evidence: One of these "erroneous renditions" turned out to be a college professor who had given an Al-Qaeda member a bad grade (the professor's name was presumably given to the CIA by the disgruntled former student).[12] About a dozen of these men have ended up at Guantánamo Bay, which a former intelligence official claimed was becoming a "dumping ground" for CIA mistakes.[13]

169

For the architects, lawyers, and managers of the CIA's Counterterrorist Center, the flexible logic of "self-defense" came to dominate the legal reasoning behind the program. In late 2002, Bush administration lawyer Jay S. Bybee had helped establish this precedent when he argued that CIA officers could torture terror suspects in the name of "self-defense." His logic, which most legal professionals found bizarre, was that a terror suspect might know of an impending attack, thus "self-defense" (of the presumed victim) dictated that torture was permitted if it might help thwart such an attack.[14] Interpreted so broadly, "self defense" becomes a euphemism for "everything is permitted."

"It's an amazing legal justification that allows them to do anything," said an unnamed official to the *Washington Post*.[15]

Even as the GST program grew, as new planes were added to classified rosters, and as fresh concrete was poured at hidden black sites, a growing number of people within the CIA began having serious misgivings about the direction of the program. Their questions were more practical than moral, revolving around the long-term wisdom of holding suspects outside of the legal system, the feasibility of maintaining a network of black sites ad infinitum, and whether intelligence officers would some day be prosecuted for the actions they'd performed on behalf of the Bush administration.

Some dissenters within the intelligence community began pointing out that once terror suspects have been held outside a legal system, it is difficult if not impossible to bring them in to the legal system. High-level terrorist suspects, for example, cannot be called as witnesses against other terror suspects in cases at home. Because they have been treated so brutally, they cannot be tried in a court in the U.S. because any evidence against them is irreparably tainted by the combination of torture and years of secret detention without access to a lawyer. Jamie Gorelick, a former deputy attorney general and member of the 9/11 Commission, articulated the paradox: "In criminal justice, you either prosecute the suspects or let them go. But if you've treated them in ways that won't *allow* you to prosecute them, you're in this no-man's land. What do you do with these people?"[16]

Other critics within the intelligence community asked about the program's sustainability: Was the CIA really going to operate a growing network of prisons around the world in perpetuity? And keep this network of prisons a secret? Would the CIA add the job of "secret jailer" to its mission?

"We never sat down, as far as I know, and came up with a grand strategy," said an unnamed intelligence officer. "Everything was very reactive. That's how you get to a situation where you pick people up, send them into a netherworld, and don't say, 'What are we going to do with them afterwards?'"[17]

171

"I kept wondering, how did we get into the prison business?" said another. "Why was the CIA doing this? This wasn't what we had been trained for."[18]

In the meantime, some CIA officers started getting worried about whether they would one day be prosecuted for interrogation techniques that the Justice Department had ruled permissible after Abu Zubayda's capture, rendition to a black site in Thailand, and torture. Although the CIA had requested—and received—detailed guidance from Alberto Gonzales' Office of Legal Council about interrogation methods, the question of being held responsible for torture began to haunt the agency. New political appointments at the Justice Department, Congressional investigations, or a turnover in the executive branch might mean that CIA officers involved in renditions and "enhanced interrogation methods" might at some point be held liable for their actions.[19] Michael Scheuer, the former head of the bin Laden unit at the Counterterrorist Center, tried to preempt any legal actions against agency officers with an editorial in the *New York Times*: "The agency is peculiarly an instrument of the executive branch," he wrote. "Renditions were called for, authorized and legally vetted not just by the NSC and the Justice Department, but also by the presidents—both Mr. Clinton and George W. Bush... if mistakes were made... the CIA officers who followed orders should not be punished."[20] In Scheuer's view, any and all blame for the rendition program, for the disappearing of prisoners, and for the prisoners' subsequent torture at the hands of U.S. officials, should be laid squarely in the President's lap.

George W. Bush was unlike other presidents, including Clinton, who had historically insulated themselves with layers of "plausible deniability" between their orders and a particular covert action. Indeed, plausible deniability has been a cornerstone of covert action since the CIA's founding in 1947. But Bush was intimately involved in the details of the program to capture, kill, render, and interrogate terror suspects. Bush famously kept a "scorecard" of captured or killed terror suspects in the top drawer of his desk—three sheets of paper with small color photographs and short bios of men he'd wanted "dead or alive." When the CIA or military captured or killed one of the men on his scorecard, Bush would put an X through their profile.[21]

The growth and continuation of the GST program was a direct result of Bush's personal commitment to it, which has counterbalanced any calls from within and outside the agency to reform the program or change its course. "In the past, presidents set up buffers to distance themselves from covert action," a former assistant general council at the CIA, A. John Radsan, told the *Washington Post.* "But this President, who is breaking down the boundaries between covert action and conventional war, seems to relish the secret findings and the dirty details of operations."[22]

Indeed, Bush's commitment hasn't wavered, and the renditions and the black sites have continued, even as the program became most visible in late 2005 and the first months of 2006. In November of 2005, Pakistani agents captured Mustafa Setmarian Nasar (whom U.S. officials suspected of being an Al-Qaeda trainer) in Quetta, Pakistan. Months later, a Pakistani intelligence official told the Associated Press that Nasar was handed over to the U.S. officials and flown "some time ago" out of Pakistan to an "undisclosed location." The United States would not confirm Nasar's apprehension, but a journalist noticed that Nasar's profile had been removed without explanation from the FBI's "Rewards for Justice" website.[23]

*   *   *

As we were finishing our work on this book, John Crewdson of the *Chicago Tribune,* citing sources close to an ongoing criminal investigation in Italy, was finally able to implicate one of the Centurion planes in a CIA kidnapping. According to Crewdson's sources, there is good evidence that Mohamed Morgan of Milan was kidnapped and flown out of Italy on a Centurion-operated plane on October 31, 2003. The CIA, it seems likely, booked Morgan a flight to Egypt on a commercial airline to cover its trail—attempting to make it look as if Morgan had traveled out of the country of his own accord. But the ruse was less than successful in that few believe Morgan left Italy on his own volition, or on that commercial flight. The lawyer listed on Braxton's corporate documents, Gary Lonergan, has refused to speak to journalists—including Crewdson and us—about the incident and has been dodging phone calls for almost a year.[24]

As we continued to monitor the Centurion planes, something else strange happened. In late June of 2006, both planes were sold. On June 21, N475LC changed hands, and N478GS followed on June 30. Both planes became the property of a company called "L-3 IS LLC." The company has a listed address in Great Falls, Montana.

The change in ownership is perhaps a dizzying distraction, but it is emblematic of the way the rendition program has been formalized under the GST: The paper trail, like the rendition flights themselves, continues.

CONCLUSION

In the end, we think back to Kabul.

We had arranged to meet Mullah Abdul Salam Zaeef at a safe house controlled by the Afghan government in the dusty outskirts of Kabul. Neighborhood children pointed us in the direction of the house, which was on a street with no name. But that's not to say that the house wasn't beautiful. Indeed, it was the nicest we'd seen during our stay in the Afghan capital. By local standards, Zaeef's lifestyle might even be described as opulent: He had a private courtyard attended by his family and associates. He could see the snowcapped mountains of Hindu Kush decorating the skyline.

Zaeef met us in a private meeting room complete with both lounge chairs for greeting Western guests and pillows for meeting frequent visitors from the Afghan provinces. Zaeef was the former Taliban Ambassador to Islamabad, a longtime supporter of Mullah Omar who had held numerous posts in the Taliban government, including minister of transportation. In the aftermath of 9/11, Zaeef had been abducted from Pakistan and branded an "enemy combatant." He had recently returned to Kabul after four years in Guantánamo Bay.

Zaeef spoke in gentle and soft-spoken English, recounting his experiences after the Taliban's fall in 2001. After taking him into custody in Peshawar, the U.S. flew him via helicopter and held him in the bowels of a Navy ship. "I don't know how many days I was there," he told us, "because I was not able to distinguish day from night." The Americans then transferred Zaeef to Bagram, then to a base outside Kandahar before finally bringing him to Guantánamo. "Not all of the soldiers were bad people," he explained about the prison, "but many of them were." Zaeef recounted incidents where American guards menaced and insulted their Islamic charges by mocking the call to prayer, by touching the prisoners' Qurans in inappropriate ways, and by threatening the prisoners with abuse. "All the time, people were trying to commit suicide... people were going insane," he told us.[1]

When the conversation turned to the history of Afghanistan and the rise and fall of the Taliban, Zaeef was silent about the relationships between the Taliban and the Al-Qaeda foreigners that his government played host to. While in power, Zaeef explained, his proudest accomplishment was to bring security to the country. "I was going to Herat without any guard or weapons," he said, and he also recalled visiting his home outside of Kandahar without a security detail, both trips that were impossibly dangerous before the Taliban's rise and which have become equally hazardous in their aftermath.

In his estimation, the Taliban's greatest mistake was its political inexperience. Their treatment of women and their disengagement from the world community came together in such a way that the regime became an easy object for the world's vilification, he thought. Zaeef did not mention Taliban support for Osama bin Laden's network as one of the regimes mistakes. According to Zaeef, one of the Taliban's greatest weaknesses was that they had needed better public relations.[2]

It was hard to sympathize with the mullah. Here was a man whose name inspired fear in the hearts of countless Afghans during the Taliban era. His government had sent citizens to hellish prisons for wearing their hair too long, donning non-traditional clothes, or refusing to grow beards. In their effort to dispel modernity from the Afghan capital, the Taliban had banned everything from leather jackets to kite-flying, and turned the city's soccer stadium into an arena for public beatings, amputations, and executions. Zaeef himself had unexplained connections to Al-Qaeda and supporters in Pakistan's infamous Inter-Services Intelligence Agency (ISI). When Pakistani terrorists kidnapped *Wall Street Journal* reporter Daniel Pearl, one of their demands was Zaeef's release in exchange for the journalist.[3]

But all of this is not the point. Indeed, our point in telling Zaeef's story is to show the complexities that the extraordinary rendition program calls forth. He reminds us that not all victims of the program are men like Khaled El-Masri, snatched from otherwise ordinary lives and thrown into the CIA's darkest dungeons, disappeared and tortured for no apparent reason. Some, like 9/11 architect Khalid Sheikh Mohammed or co-conspirator Ramzi bin al-Shibh, are unquestionably cruel and despicable.

Nonetheless, when one is talking about disappearing people, about torturing people, about holding people incommunicado at secret locations throughout the world, one cannot make sensible distinctions between innocence and guilt. Those are legal terms, and in a world of black sites, disappearances, waterboarding, Salt Pits, and Dark Prisons, words like guilt and innocence are misapplied. Indeed, in the absence of law, guilt and innocence become meaningless, even misleading.

All of this, of course, points to the crucial and corrupting consequences of the extraordinary rendition program, for the legalistic and moral assumptions underlying the program sculpt a world in which everything is permitted.

*   *   *

In June of 2006, Swiss Senator Dick Marty filed a report on extraordinary rendition for the Council of Europe's Parliamentary Assembly. The report had been commissioned in late 2005 after mounting evidence suggested that many European countries had quietly participated in the rendition program through active cooperation or passive acquiescence to the United States' wishes. After seven months of research, requesting information from European Union member states, interviews with journalists and former CIA agents, and testimony from victims of the rendition program, Marty concluded that "most governments did not seem particularly eager to establish the alleged facts." Rather, Marty reported the facts "[make] it unlikely that European states were completely unaware of what was happening, in the context of the fight against international terrorism, in some of their airports, in their airspace or at American bases located on this territory." He concluded "Insofar as they did not know, they did not want to know. It is inconceivable that certain operations conducted by American services could have taken place without the active participation, or at least the collusion, of national intelligence services."[4]

183

Senator Marty's investigation had been narrowly defined: He sought only specific information about whether and how European states had participated in the extraordinary rendition program. But his findings were expansive, revealing that the torture planes had crisscrossed Europe and the world, touching down on numerous airstrips in countries including: Afghanistan, Algeria, Australia, Azerbaijan, Bahrain, Columbia, Croatia, Cyprus, Czech Republic, Djibouti, Egypt, Estonia, Fiji, Germany, Greece, Iraq, Ireland, Italy, Jordan, Kuwait, Libya, Macedonia, Malta, Morocco, Pakistan, Poland, Portugal, Romania, Russia, Saudi Arabia, Spain, Sudan, Sweden, Switzerland, Tajikistan, Turks and Caicos Islands, the United Arab Emirates, United Kingdom, United States of America, and Uzbekistan.[5]

In addition to the Council of Europe investigation, there was also another high-profile investigation, in Italy. There, government prosecutors had learned of the kidnapping of Osama Nasr Mostafa Hassan, known as Abu Omar, from Milan by the CIA. Twenty CIA agents were said to be involved. The first group of agents, a surveillance team, arrived in the early days of January 2003 and left a big trail. Some of the agents took up residence at the Principe di Savoia, where a single room costs $588 per night. Before the end of their stay, the CIA had billed American taxpayers over $39,995 for the rooms at the Principe di Savoia, while another group of operatives put $40,098 on the American tab for a stay at the Westin Palace, another luxury hotel. By the end of the operation, the group had paid $158,096.56 in room charges, and gone on weekend getaways to Florence and the Mediterranean coast.[6]

On Monday, February 17, 2003, CIA agents snatched Abu Omar as he left his apartment en route to a local mosque. His kidnappers sprayed a chemical in his face and stuffed him into a white van.

From there, the plot thickened. Abu Omar was, it turned out, a former CIA operative himself, and his former employer was giving him a choice: Restart his relationship with the agency, or face torture in an Egyptian prison. Abu Omar was flown out of Italy on a military Learjet and then transferred, at the U.S. Air Force Base in Ramstein, Germany, to the notorious Red Sox Gulfstream, and flown to Egypt. In Egypt, Omar wasn't feeling cooperative. He refused the offer to become an agent or informer, and disappeared into an Egyptian prison.[7]

Immediately after Omar's disappearance in February 2003, Italian anti-terrorism police—who had, it turned out, been keeping Omar under their own surveillance—started frantically searching for him. The CIA reported to the Italian police that they had "good information" indicating that the imam had fled to the Balkans. It was a deliberate lie, designed to throw Italian police off the CIA's trail—and it worked, at least for a while. But when Italian police intercepted a telephone call Abu Omar made to his wife (during a brief release in April 2004), they realized that the CIA had misled them. Their missing persons investigation thundered back to life, and the CIA found itself under the scrutiny of an Italian prosecutor named Armando Sparato.[8]

In the summer of 2005, Sparato began issuing arrest warrants for the suspected kidnappers: CIA agents, many of whom the prosecutor only knew by their aliases. By the end of 2005, Sparato had EU-wide warrants for 22 Americans accused of kidnapping Abu Omar. The following year, four more American names were added to the list.

For coordinating the kidnapping, the Italian prosecutor issued a warrant for a man named Robert Seldon Lady, the CIA's substation chief in Milan.[9] Italian investigators had searched Lady's home outside Milan and found a disk with a digital photograph of Abu Omar at the place where he was kidnapped, which indicated that Lady had been involved in Omar's kidnapping. The Italians also noticed that Lady had booked himself a plane ticket from Zurich to Cairo five days after Abu Omar's abduction. Lady stayed in Cairo for three weeks, leading the prosecutors to conclude that Lady was present during Omar's initial interrogations.[10]

But by the time Sparato's arrest warrants came through, the CIA officers were long gone and unlikely to return. On December 24, 2004, they had received emails with the subject "Italy, don't go there." The email, sent from the CIA to operatives involved in the Omar abduction, arrived when the agency learned of Italian intentions to arrest the agents.[11]

Meanwhile, as Sparato's investigation progressed, things got more interesting: The prosecutor was uncovering more and more evidence of Italian cooperation with the kidnapping. Italian officials categorically denied any involvement or knowledge about Abu Omar's rendition, but when the case started to become public, CIA operatives involved in the abduction told their superiors that the kidnapping had been cleared by the Italian military intelligence agency and, ultimately, with the consent of none other than Italian Prime Minister Silvio Berlusconi. Other surprising details also began to emerge: An Italian police officer going by the code name "Ludwig" admitted to prosecutors that he'd been directly involved in the kidnapping. In light of the evidence of a high-level collaboration between states, it seems that the operation may have been "some of the most sensitive stuff not on paper," as Bush had called operations authorized after September 2001. If Berlusconi was involved, it's likely that he demanded "plausible deniability." A former intelligence official said in reference to the case:"The price of doing business is if you get caught, you're on your own."[12]

On July 5, 2006 Italian police arrested two senior members of SISMI, the Italian military counterespionage agency, accusing the men of helping to plan and execute the kidnapping. Taken into custody were Marco Mancini, the head of SISMI, and Gustavo Pignero, Mancini's predecessor and SISMI chief at the time of Abu Omar's kidnapping. As a part of their investigation, the Italian police had placed wiretaps on intelligence agents' phones. On July 1, 2006 the two spies appeared to have slipped up. Pignero called Mancini from a public phone and told his colleague that he'd admitted to prosecutors that "Yankee" agents had asked SISMI to "identify and check out" the imam. The two Italian spies went on to discuss the fact that they knew the Americans actually wanted to kidnap Omar. The intercepted conversation convinced Sparato's prosecutors that the men had advance knowledge of—and cooperated with—Abu Omar's kidnapping.[13] Sparato's office indicated that more arrests might be on the way: by analyzing cell phones involved in the abduction, the prosecutor concluded that still more Italian agents may have been involved.[14]

*   *   *

Sparato's long investigation and Swiss Senator Marty's Council of Europe report contrast starkly with the U.S. government's response to a long series of disclosures about the rendition program. The administration argued that torture, a key component of extraordinary rendition, was an important tool in the "war on terror," and when Senator John McCain sought to unequivocally ban the use of torture, the Bush administration was openly hostile to the proposal.

Once the bill containing McCain's anti-torture amendment had passed, Vice President Dick Cheney went to work behind the scenes trying to create loopholes: He wanted the CIA exempt from the proposed law, and wanted to do away with the Army Field Manual requirements for the Defense Department.[15] The Bush administration was eventually forced to accept the bill with McCain's amendment attached after it passed with veto-proof majorities in both houses.

But even as Congress passed the law designed to prohibit torture, President Bush added a "signing statement" to the bill in which he made his intentions clear: "The executive branch shall construe [the law] in a manner consistent with the constitutional authority of the President to supervise the unitary executive branch and as Commander in Chief and consistent with the constitutional limitations on the judicial power."[16] In other words, Bush claimed that he did not have to actually abide by the new law: His power as "Commander in Chief" and the power of the "unitary executive branch" overrode the law. In essence, in its handling of the McCain amendment, the Bush administration admitted that it had been ignoring the law, that it planned to continue to do so, and most astoundingly, that it had a legitimate right to ignore congressional and constitutional checks on executive power.

While the Bush administration battled congress over its attempt to ban torture, Congress began a campaign of retribution against people it suspected of leaking the administration's secrets about the rendition program to the public. When Dana Priest's article about the Bush administration's network of black sites was published in the *Washington Post* in November 2005, Congress' reaction was not to launch an investigation, nor to demand accountability from the administration, nor did they attempt to ban the practice of "disappearing" people into hidden dungeons. Instead, Congress' fury was directed at the unnamed source of this information: the "leaker." When Senator Bill Frist and House Speaker J. Dennis Hastert wrote that the revelations "could have long-term and far-reaching damaging and dangerous consequences," they were not writing about the secret prisons, the acts of torture, or the illegal extraordinary renditions: They were writing about a threat to "national security" that did not come from these practices but rather came from airing them in public.

Rage against the "leaker" also came from the executive branch. White House Press Secretary Scott McClellan said: "I think that you've heard [the President] express his views: the leaking of classified information is a serious matter and ought to be taken seriously." The Bush administration then proceeded to launch a series of internal investigations designed to ferret out officials who had leaked information about the extraordinary rendition program and the black sites. CIA agents were forced to undergo polygraph examinations about their relationships to journalists. In April 2006, the CIA fired Mary O. McCarthy for having undisclosed contact with journalists in violation of the CIA's secrecy agreement. McCarthy denied that she had a role in leaking classified information.[17] What's more the administration indicated that it might be willing to go much further to stop leaks to the press—journalists might become their next targets. The Justice Department issued warnings that it might start prosecuting journalists using archaic espionage laws.

In the meantime, the administration was resorting to a previously-obscure "state secrets" doctrine in defending itself from lawsuits brought by two victims of extraordinary rendition, Maher Arar and the aforementioned Khalid al-Masri, both of whom were abducted, disappeared, and tortured at the CIA's behest. The Department of Justice did not try to defend the practice or even question whether the renditions had happened. Instead, it invoked the "states secrets" privilege to preempt a discovery process. Essentially, the Department of Justice argued that if the lawsuits were allowed to proceed, they would cause exceptional harm to national security, even if all of the relevant parties were granted security clearances and the trial was not public. The state secrets privilege is "absolute," wrote Justice Department lawyers on behalf of the Bush administration, "including in cases alleging constitutional violations."[18]

Compared with the Italian investigation of Abu Omar's abduction and the Council of Europe's report, U.S. oversight and investigation of the extraordinary rendition program is certainly marginal, and there are clear reasons for this, reasons tightly connected to the Bush's administration's expansive views of executive power. The extraordinary rendition program goes to the heart of questions about Presidential powers, the exercise of said powers, and the continued use of those powers. On one hand, to claim an inherent authority to torture, as the Bush administration's lawyers have done, is in practice to reject any checks on Presidential power. Because prohibitions against torture form the bedrock of human rights in both domestic and international law, to reject this prohibition is to reject the law entirely. Indeed, the extraordinary rendition program, perhaps more than any other single program, is central to the administration's implementation of its "New Paradigm" and their vision of a "unitary executive" able to act unilaterally in areas of defense.

Perhaps all of this is best illustrated by a December 2005 debate between former Bush administration lawyer John Yoo and Doug Cassel of Notre Dame Law School, wherein Cassel asked: "If the President deems that he's got to torture somebody, including by crushing the testicles of the person's child, there is no law that can stop him?"

"No treaty," came Yoo's response.

"Also, no law by Congress—that is what you wrote in the August 2002 memo," added Cassel.

"I think it depends on why the President thinks he needs to do that," Yoo concluded.

Interpreting all of this, Bruce Fein, a Republican legal activist, summarized: "If you used the President's reasoning, you could shut down Congress for leaking too much... he could kill someone in Lafayette Park if he wants!"[19]

*   *   *

In concluding a book such as this one, it's customary to offer clichés about the importance of more open pubic debate, or to offer glimmers of hope, rays of light at the end of a dark tunnel. Unfortunately, we cannot do that. The facts show that the U.S. has become a nation that disappears people and practices torture. What's more, the torture planes, the renditions, and the executive orders that produced them seem here to stay.

And so we find ourselves in a position not unlike those who first noticed a constellation of unusual aircraft at Desert Rock Airstrip back in December of 2002. They saw four planes. Two—the Hercules and the Cessna—represented the continuing secret wars of the past. Two others—the "737 Boeing Business Jet" and the "Red Sox" Gulfstream—represented a hidden present and an unresolved future. As we take account of these aircraft, of the disappearances and torture that they have come to represent, of the horror stories they have helped to reveal and those that undoubtedly remain obscure, one thing remains to be seen. Do the aircraft, with their bone-white exteriors, ever-changing registration numbers, and visits to "lots of interesting places"—in the euphemistic words of a planespotter who first began tracking their movements—represent a tentative glimpse into a disconcerting past, or do they, in fact, mark the beginnings of a long and unsettling future?

I. THE PROGRAM

1   Dick Marty, "Alleged secret detentions and unlawful inter-state transfers involving Council of Europe member states," Council of Europe, Committee on Legal Affairs and Human Rights, Explanatory Memorandum, June 7, 2006, p. 45.

2   Diary of Binyam Mohammed Al Habashi, a document supplied by Mohammed's lawyer, Clive Stafford Smith.

3   Ibid.

4   Bob Woodward, *Bush At War* (New York: Simon & Schuster, 2002), pp. 76-78.

5   Ibid., pp. 76-77.

6   Transcript of Vice President Cheney on NBC's *Meet the Press*, September 16, 2001, available at: www.washingtonpost.com/wp-srv/nation/attacked/tran-scripts/cheney091601.html

7   Kamran Khan and Rajiv Chandrasekaran, "Cole Suspect Turned Over by Pakistan," *Washington Post*, October 28, 2001, A01. See also Dana Priest, "Jet is Open Secret in Terror War," *Washington Post*, December 27, 2004, A01.

8   Dana Priest, "Al Qaeda Link Recanted; Captured Libyan Reverses Previous Statement to CIA, Officials Say," *Washington Post*, August 1, 2004, A20.

9   Bradley Graham and Walter Pincus, "Al Qaeda Trainer in U.S. Hands," *Washington Post*, January 5, 2002, A01. See also Center for Human Rights and Global Justice, *Fate and Whereabouts Unknown: Detainees in the "War on Terror"* (New York: NYU School of Law, 2005). Available at nyuhr.org/docs/Whereabouts%20Unknown%20Final.pdf

10 Kamran Khan and Rajiv Chandrasekaran. "Cole Suspect Turned Over by Pakistan."

11 Rajiv Chandrasekaran and Peter Finn, "U.S. Behind Secret Transfer of Terror Suspects," *Washington Post,* March 11, 2002, A01.

12 See The Committee on International Human Rights of the Association of the Bar of the City of New York and the Center for Global Justice and Human Rights, New York Law School, *Torture By Proxy: International and Domestic Law Applicable to "Extraordinary Renditions"* (New York: NYU Law School, 2004).

13 Diary of Binyam Mohammed Al Habashi. Binyam Mohammed's account was reprinted in the *Daily Mail*, December 11, 2005. Available at www.dailymail.co.uk/pages/live/articles/news/news.html?in_article_id=371330&in_page_id=1770 accessed 06/06/2006. (Accessed 6/6/2006).

14 Ibid.

15 Ibid.

16 Ibid.

17 Ibid.

18 Ibid.

19 See Neil Lewis, "Yemini Held in Guantánamo was Seized in Cario, Group Says," *New York Times*, March 30, 2005.

20 Diary of Binyam Mohammed.

21 Ibid.

22 Ibid.

23 Ibid.

24 Jane Mayer, "Outsourcing Torture: The Secret History of America's 'Extraordinary Rendition' Program," *New Yorker*, February 14, 2005. See also Alfred McCoy, *A Question of Torture: CIA Interrogation, from the Cold War to the War on Terror* (New York: Metropolitan Books, 2006), p. 118.

25 Jane Mayer, "Outsourcing Torture."

26 Dana Priest, "Al Qaeda Link Recanted."

27 Ron Suskind, *The One Percent Doctrine* (New York: Simon and Schuster, 2006), p. 95.

28 Ibid., p.100.

29 David Johnston and James Risen, "Aides Say Memo Backed Coercion Already in Use," *New York Times,* June 27, 2004; Also McCoy, p. 121-122; and Mark Danner, *Torture and Truth* (New York: New York Review Books, 2004), p. 115-166.

30 Suskind, pp. 100-101.

31 James Risen, *State of War* (New York: The Free Press, 2006), p. 23.

32 See McCoy, p. 121; and Suskind, p. 115.

33 Suskid, p. 115.

34 Jane Mayer, "Outsourcing Torture."

35 See www.defenselink.mil/news/Nov2005/d20051104muhammad.pdf

36 See *United States of America v. Binyam Ahmed Muhammad.*Online at: *www.defenselink.mil/news/Nov2005/d20051104muhammad.pdf*

37 See The Committee on International Human Rights of the Association of the Bar of the City of New York, *Torture By Proxy.*

38 Quoted in Seymour Hersh, *Chain of Command* (New York: HarperCollins, 2004), p. 18.

II. TRACKING THE TORTURE PLANES
CHAPTER ONE *PAPER AIRPLANES*

1   Victor Marchetti and John D. Marks, *The CIA and the Cult of Intelligence* (New York: Alfred A. Knopf, 1974), p. 134.
2   Ibid.
3   Ibid., p. 135.
4   Ben Rich and Leo Janos, *Skunk Works* (Boston: Little Brown and Company, 1994), p. 120.
5   Ibid, p. 133.
6   See Francis Gary Powers with Curt Gentry, *Operation Overflight* (New York: Holt, Rinehart and Winston, 1970).
7   Walter Pincus and Mike Allen, "Leak of Agent's Name Causes Exposure of CIA Front Firm," *Washington Post,* October 4, 2003, A03.
8   Certifications of Incorporation for Crowell Aviation Technologies and Premier Executive Transport Services, filed with the State of Delaware Secretary of State on January 10, 1994.
9   Professional bio of Ralph Kissick available at www.zsrlaw.com/attorneys/atty_bios/rlk.htm (accessed 3/14/2006).
10 See *Recon/Optical, Inc. v. Government of Israel*, United States Court of Appeals for the Second Cirtuit, 816 F.2d 854; 1987 U.S. App. LEXIS 5217; 3 U.C.C. Rep. Serv. 2d (Callaghan) 1860.
11 See Kissick's online biography.
12 Dana Priest, "Jet is Open Secret in Terror War."
13 Corporate records from these companies are on file with the Secretary of States of Maryland, Delaware, Tennessee, and Massachusetts. Additional documents connecting these various people, places, and companies come from records on file with the Federal Aviation Administration.
14 See "Flight Logs related to the Successive Rendition Operations of Binyam Mohammed and Khaled El-Masri in January 2004," Council of Europe Report, Appendix No. 1.
15 Information culled from Federal Aviation Administration registration histories and airworthiness documents for the Gulfstream.
16 Ibid.
17 We are relying here on airworthiness records from the FAA.
18 Kamran Khan and Rajiv Chandrasekaran, "Cole Suspect Turned Over by Pakistan." Also Dana Priest, "Jet is Open Secret in Terror War."
19 See Rajiv Chandrasekaran and Peter Finn, "U.S. Behind Secret Transfer of Terror Suspects."
20 Kamran Khan and Rajiv Chandrasekaran. "Cole Suspect Turned Over by Pakistan;" also Dana Priest, "Jet is Open Secret in Terror War."
21 See Callum Macdonald, "Bush Backs Call to Outlaw Torture as CIA Rendition Flights in Scotland are Confirmed," *The Herald (Glasgow)*, December 16, 2005, p. 5.
22 See transcript of "The Broken Promise I," *Kalla Fakta*, Swedish TV4, May 17, 2004; and "The Broken Promise II," *Kalla Fakta*, Swedish TV4, May 24, 2004. See also Craig Whitlock, "New Swedish Documents Illuminate CIA Action; Probe Finds 'Rendition' of Terror Suspects Illegal," *Washington Post*, May 21, 2005, A01.

23 Ibid.

24 Ibid.

25 Ibid.

26 Ibid.

27 See Seymour Hersh, *Chain of Command*, p. 54.

28 See "Broken Promise I;" and Farah Stockman, "Terror Suspects' Torture Claims Have Mass. Link," *Boston Globe,* November 29, 2004.

29 See "Broken Promise I."

30 See, for example, Joanne Omang, "Shultz Bids Public Air Terrorism Fight; Secretary Seeking a National Consensus," *Washington Post*, October 26, 1984, A1.

31 Report of the National Commission on Terrorist Attacks on the United States, *The 9/11 Commission Report* (New York: W.W. Norton and Company), p. 75.

32 Steve Coll, *Ghost Wars: The Secret History of the CIA, Afghanistan, and Bin Laden, from the Soviet Invasion to September 10, 2001* (New York: The Penguin Press, 2004), p. 378.

33 *9/11 Commission Report*, p. 92.

34 See Steve Coll, *Ghost Wars,* pp. 272-275. See also Alfred McCoy, *A Question of Torture*, pp. 110-112; also Christopher Wren, "Verdicts in Terror Trial: The Overview; U.S. Jury Convicts 3 in a Conspiracy to Bomb Airliners," *Washington Post*, September 6, 1996; A01.

35 See Paul R. Pillar, *Terrorism and U.S. Foreign Policy* (Washington D.C.: Brookings Institution Press, 2001), pp. 117-118.

36 Jane Mayer, "Outsourcing Torture."

37 Ibid.

38 "Written Statement for the Record of the Director of Central Intelligence Before the National Commission on Terrorist Attacks Upon the United States, March 24, 2004." See also, "Below the Radar: Secret Flights to Torture and 'Disappearance,'" Amnesty International Report. Available at web.amnesty.org/library/index/ENGAMR510512006 (accessed 6/3/2006).

39 Jane Mayer, "Outsourcing Torture."

40 Michael Scheuer, "A Fine Rendition," *New York Times*, March 11, 2005, p. 23.

41 Pillar, p. 118.

42 See "Written Statement for the Record of the Director of Central Intelligence, October 17, 2002."

43 Statement of Cofer Black, Joint Investigation into September 11, September 26, 2002.

44 For documents relating to the Chicago Convention, see the website for the International Civil Aviation Organization at www.icao.int. The specifics of the Chicago Convention are at www.icao.int/icaonet/dcs/7300.html (accessed 6/16/2006).

45 Interview with Farah Stockman, March 3, 2006.

46 Ibid.

CHAPTER TWO *A TOWN CALLED SMITHFIELD*

1 Interview with Allyson and Walt Caison, Smithfield, North Carolina, April 13, 2006.
2 Ibid.
3 Interview with Jordan Cooke, April 14, 2006. See also Jordan Cook, "Aero Denies CIA Flight," *The Herald (Smithfield – Clayton – Cleveland)*, March 11, 2005.
4 Scott Shane, Stephen Grey, and Margot Williams, "CIA Expanding Terror Battle Under Guise of Charter Flights," *New York Times*, May 31, 2005.
5 See Federal Aviation Administration files on Boeing Business Jet N4476S, serial number 33010; and FAA files for N4476S, Gulfstream V, serial number 581.
6 See John Prados, *President's Secret Wars* (Chicago: Ivan R. Dee, 1996), pp. 62-64. See also William Leary, *Perilous Missions* (University: University of Alabama Press, 1984).
7 See John Prados, *President's Secret Wars*, pp. 98-106. See also Nick Cullather, *Secret History: The CIA's Classified Account of its Operations in Guatemala 1952-1954* (Stanford: Stanford University Press, 1999).
8 Prados, p. 231.
9 Ibid., p. 184.
10 Kevin O'Brien, "Interfering with Civil Society: CIA and KGB Covert Political Action during the Cold War," *International Journal of Intelligence and Counterintelligence*, 1995, Vol. 8, Issue 4.
11 See for example Peter Dale Scott and Jonathan Marshall, *Cocaine Politics* (Berkeley: University of California Press, 1998), p. 18.
12 Prados, pp. 324-325
13 See Prados, pp. 374-375. See also Lawrence E. Walsh *Firewall* (New York: Norton, 1997), pp. 74-75. For Tepper Aviation, see Ted Gup, *The Book of Honor* (New York: Doubleday, 2000), p. 330.
14 For a brief history of Jim Rhyne's Air American career, see Ted Gup, *The Book of Honor*, pp. 245-246.
15 Interview with former Aero Contractors pilot.
16 Ibid.
17 Ibid.
18 FAA registration and airworthiness records for N168D, N4476S, and other aircraft.
19 Sam Atkins,"Global TransPark Board Approves Operating Budget," *Goldsboro News-Argus*, June 23, 2004.
20 Ibid. See also Monica Chen, "Protest Ends in Arrests," *The Herald (Smithfield – Clayton – Cleveland),* November 22, 2005.

CHAPTER THREE PLANESPOTTING

1   Interviews with planespotters.
2   Ibid.
3   Ibid.
4   The ACARS message was posted on the Luchtzak Aviation forum at
    www.luchtzak.be/postt6528.html (accessed 06/13/2006).
5   Ibid.
6   Ibid.
7   Multiple interviews with "Ray." March–June 2006.
8   See "DEPARTMENT OF THE INTERIOR, Bureau of Land Management, 43 CFR
    Public Land Order 6591, [N-35951], Nevada; Withdrawal of Land for Air
    Force Communication Site," Bureau of Land Management, Interior. ACTION:
    Public Land Order. Federal Register / Vol. 50, No. 53 / Tuesday, March 19,
    1985 / Page 10965. (50 FR 10965).
9   Multiple interviews with "Ray." March – June 2006.
10 Ibid.
11 Ibid.
12 The CALP is available at www.usaasa.belvoir.army.mil/CALP/CALPDec05.htm
    (accessed 6/6/2006). Previous versions of the CALP area available at the
    Internet Archive, www.archive.org (accessed 6/6/2006).
13 Interview with John Sifton, New York, New York, April 6, 2006.
14 Ibid.
15 See Amnesty International, "Below the Radar: Secret Flights to Torture and
    Disappearance."
16 Ibid.
17 Ibid.
18 Ibid.
19 Ibid.
20 Brian Ross and Richard Esposito, "Sources Tell ABC News Top Al-Qaeda
    Figures Held in Secret CIA Prisons," *ABC News*, December 5, 2005.
21 See the Brian Ross Podcast from December 5, 2005. The Podcast confirmed
    that Poland had housed a black site on its territory. CIA officials successfully
    pressured ABC News to refrain from naming Poland on the evening's news
    program. See also Brian Ross and Richard Esposito, "Sources Tell ABC
    News."
22 See Amnesty Report.
23 Interview with Stephen Grey, June 2, 2006.
24 Gerard Seenan and Giles Tremlett, "How Planespotters Turned into the Scourge
    of the CIA," *The Guardian*, December 10, 2005.
25 Ibid.
26 Ibid.
27 Ibid.

CHAPTER FOUR *DARK PRISONS*

1   Prisoner accounts provided by Clive Stafford Smith's office.
2   See Dana Priest, "CIA Holds Terror Suspects in Secret Prisons," *Washington Post*, November 2, 2005, A01.
3   Dana Priest, "CIA Holds Terror Suspects in Secret Prisons." See also Dana Priest, "CIA Avoids Scrutiny of Detainee Treatment; Afghan Death Took Two Years to Come to Light; Agency Says Abuse Claims Are Probed Fully," *Washington Post*, March 3, 2005, A01.
4   Dana Priest, "CIA Holds Terror Suspects."
5   Carlotta Gall, "Study Hints at Mass Killings of the Taliban," *New York Times*, May 1, 2002, p. 8.
6   Dana Priest, "CIA Avoids Scrutiny."
7   "Declaration of Khaled El-Masri in Support of Plaintiff's Opposition to the United States' Motion to Dismiss or, in the Alternative, for Summary Judgement," *Khaled El-Masri v. George Tenet, et. al.* Civil Action No. 1:05cv1417-TSE-TRJ. El-Masri's statement is originally written in German—direct quotes are from the English translation provided in the court documents. In some cases, we had relied on El-Masri's original statement in German when it contained untranslated details.
8   Ibid.
9   Ibid.
10 Ibid.
11 Interview with Dr. Rafiullah Bidar, Gardez, May 21, 2006.
12 Ibid.
13 Ibid.
14 Interview with Allah Noor, Gardez, May 21, 2006.
15 Ibid.
16 Ibid.
17 Ibid.
18 Ibid.
19 Ibid.
20 Interview with Gannat Gul, Gardez, May 21, 2006.
21 Ibid.
22 Ibid.
23 Ibid.

CHAPTER FIVE RENDITION NOW

1   History culled from registration documents for both aircraft on file with the
    Federal Aviation Administration.
2   See John Crewdson, "Mysterious Jet Tied to Torture Flights: Is Shadowy Firm a
    Front for CIA?" *Chicago Tribune*, January 8, 2005, p. 1. See also Josef
    Schneider, "Torture from Above," *Portland Mercury*, March 31-April 6, 2005.
3   See AC Thompson and Trevor Paglen, "The CIA's Torture Taxi," *Reno News and
    Review*, December 29, 2005.
4   Web history from www.usaircraftsales.com/forsale.html (accessed 6/9/2006).
5   Brian Ross and Richard Esposito, "Sources Tell ABC News."
6   Sources on planespotting websites.
7   Human Rights Watch, "U.S. Operated Secret 'Dark Prison' in Kabul," December
    19, 2005. Available at hrw.org/english/docs/2005/12/19/afghan12319.htm
    (accessed 5/11/2006).
8   Tom Walker and Sarah Baxter, "Revealed: The Terror Prison U.S. is Helping to
    Build in Morocco," *Sunday Times,* February 12, 2006. Available at
    www.timesonline.co.uk/article/0,,2089-2036185.html (accessed 5/11/2006).
9   Dana Priest, "Covert CIA Program Withstands New Furor; Anti-Terror Effort
    Continues to Grow," *Washington Post*, December 30, 2005, A01.
10 Ibid.
11 Dana Priest, "CIA Holds Terror Suspects in Secret Prisons."
12 Dana Priest, "Wrongful Imprisonment: Anatomy of a CIA Mistake," *Washington
    Post,* December 4, 2005, A01.
13 Ibid.
14 See Mark Danner, *Torture and Truth*, pp. 153-154.
15 Dana Priest, "Covert CIA Program."
16 Jane Mayer, "Outsourcing Torture."
17 Dana Priest, "CIA Holds Terror Suspects in Secret Prisons."
18 James Risen, *State of War*, p. 31.
19 Douglas Jehl and David Johnston, "Within the CIA, Growing Fears of
    Prosecution," *New York Times*, February 27, 2005.
20 Michael Scheuer, "A Fine Rendition."
21 Dan Balz and Bob Woodward, "Bush Awaits History's Judgment," *Washington
    Post*, February 3, 2002, A01.
22 Dana Priest, "Covert CIA Program."
23 Associated Press, "Top Al-Qaida Leader Nasar Captured in Pakistan," May 2,
    2006.
24 John Crewdson, "CIA targeted 'more than 10' in Italy for kidnap, agent says,"
    Chicago Tribune, July 31, 2006.

CONCLUSION

1   Interview with Mullah Zaeef, Kabul, May 20, 2006.
2   Ibid.
3   See Bernard-Henri Lévy, *Who Killed Daniel Pearl?* (Hoboken: Melville House, 2004).
4   Dick Marty, "Alleged Secret Detentions and Unlawful Inter-State Transfers Involving Council of Europe Member States," p. 50.
5   List of countries provided by Amnesty International and private sources. See "Below the Radar: Secret flights to torture and 'disappearance.'"
6   John Crewdson, "CIA team traveled Italy in Style," *Chicago Tribune*, December 25, 2005, p. 14.
7   Ibid.
8   Craig Whitlock, "CIA Ruse is Said to Have Damaged Probe in Milan; Italy Allegedly Misled on Cleric's Abduction," *Washington Post,* December 6, 2005, A01.
9   Names reproduced here have been published numerous times in Italian news-papers. See for example, www.dsmilano.it/html/Pressroom/2005/06/cor5_0629_commando-cia-i-nomi.htm
10   Craig Whitlock, "CIA Ruse is Said to Have Damaged Probe in Milan."
11   John Crewdson, "Italy: CIA e-mail ties agents to abduction," *Chicago Tribune*, January 20, 2006.
12   Craig Whitlock, "CIA Ruse is said to Have Damaged Probe in Milan."
13   Stephen Grey and Elisabetta Povoledo, "Inquiry in 2003 Abduction Rivets Italy," *New York Times*, July 8, 2006.
14   Ibid.
15   Jeffrey R. Smith and Josh White, "Cheney Plan Exempts CIA From Bill Barring Abuse of Detainees," *Washington Post*, October 25, 2005, A01.
16   For the full text of the signing statement, see the White House website at: www.whitehouse.gov/news/releases/2005/12/20051230-8.html.
17   Jeffrey Smith and Dafna Linzer, "Dismissed CIA Officer Denies Leak Role," *Washington Post*, April 25, 2006, A01.
18   See "Reply of United States of American to Plaintiff's Opposition to United States' Invocation of State Secrets Privilege," *Maher Arar v. Ashcroft et. al.* Case No. 04-CV-0249-DGT-VVP, April 4, 2005.
19   Jane Mayer, "The Hidden Power," *New Yorker*, July 3, 2006.

ACKNOWLEDGEMENTS

The authors would like foremost to acknowledge the financial and technical support of Sandy Close and New America Media, whose backing made our overseas reporting possible. Without Close and her colleagues, our journey to Afghanistan, which was key to this book, would not have been possible. We would also like to thank the Paglen clan, the Thompson clan, Allan Pred, Ananya Roy, Praba Pilar, Gillian Hart, Ruth Wilson Gilmore, LPS, Maiwand Mrowat, and Kelly Burdick and Melville House.

A NOTE ON THE REPORTING

The "we" voice is used throughout the text for consistency, though we did some of the reporting as a team and some of it separately. For the record: Thompson and Paglen reported from Smithfield, North Carolina; Reno, Nevada; northern California, including the East Bay suburbs and the area around Beale Air Force Base; and Kabul, Afghanistan. Paglen reported from New York City, and Dedham, Massachusetts. Thompson reported from Gardez, Afghanistan.